WITHDRAWN

Between the Lines
Reflections on War and Peacetime

L. William Cracken
Colonel, USAF (Ret.)

Taylor Publishing Company
Dallas, Texas

First to my son, John, who inspired me to write this book, and then my wife, Marilyn, daughter, Rachel, and her husband, Paul. To John's wife, Heather (known to the children as "BB"), and all of my grandchildren—Robert, William, Eric, Marilyn, and John's and Heather's soon-to-be-born son, Preston.

Contents

Acknowledgments

I would like to thank the following individuals who contributed to this project: First and foremost, my son, John, who was the instigator; my son-in-law, Paul Herbig, who wrote the first draft; my wife, Marilyn, and daughter, Rachel, who kept pushing me to do this for my children and grandchildren every time I said forget it; and, finally, Sally Giddens Stephenson, a professional writer who helped me tell these stories. I would also like to acknowledge Colonel Ellis Vander Pyl, a gentleman, patriot, and professional who was a positive and caring influence throughout my career.

A Soldier's Story

Introduction

I never would have written this book if it weren't for relentless urging by my son, John, and daughter, Rachel. In fact, it was only after John insisted he would do it without me, using the audiotapes I had recorded, that I gave in and agreed to help a professional writer get it done.

The stories themselves are worth telling, particularly those about the military government in Korea, where I was in 1946 and 1947. Very little has been written about this period in American history during which a handful of dedicated Americans managed millions of Koreans and worked to get Korea running again. The only other major similar period in our country's history was the American occupation of the Philippines after the Spanish-American War. The military government in Europe after World War II was significantly different. There we dealt with a defeated nation, whereas in the Philippines and Korea, we dealt with colonial countries we had liberated from two former enemies. In Korea, we didn't have the same authority. Also, the European culture was more familiar to Americans than the Korean culture.

Introduction

In the Philippines and in Korea, we strengthened both a devastated economy and a fragile alliance. I am happy to be able to shed some light on the Korean experience and recognize the important efforts of the American military—both officers and enlisted men. All you have to do is look at the marked differences between South Korea and North Korea today to know that the American military government did something very right. Our success actually contributed to the Korean War because efforts by the Soviets and Chinese to subvert our thriving system fell short. Today, South Korea is an economic power whose roots can be traced directly to the democracy we established and nurtured.

Initially, I told these stories to my son-in-law, Paul, with audiotapes as backup, and later to a professional writer, Sally Giddens Stephenson, who took the project a step further. Together, I hope we have captured the excitement and flavor of some unique times in world history. The people and names in this book are all real. In some cases, when it was appropriate or when I couldn't remember, I have omitted names. These experiences have shaped my philosophy, and, by sharing them, I hope others will gain an even deeper awareness of the meaning of life.

I selected only incidents I felt appropriate, omitting really personal experiences and making judgments of other people, not usually knowing all of the facts. It was difficult to select a limited number of photographs and documents from my files. I tried to pick those that most closely supported the book. I regret that I lost or threw away almost all references to my life before the Korean Military Government period, and quite a few after that period as well.

It's important to understand that the perspective in this book is that of a soldier not a hero. I was a decorated officer, but I don't cherish those decorations, and I don't like the idea of them being used to glorify war. Decorations are necessary for morale, but the reality is that some people get them who don't deserve them and others don't get them who do. Truthfully, the real war heroes, those who deserve the highest honors, are the people who are killed, seriously wounded, or disabled.

I spent a lifetime in service to this country. What I learned and what many people don't realize is that war not only kills and hurts the young men who are fighting, but little children and women—human beings who are totally innocent and just happen to be caught between the two opposing forces.

During World War II, I was in the jungle in the South Pacific, which obscured many of the atrocities of combat. But in Korea, both during the time of the military government and later during the Korean War, the little children bearing the scars of battle were all around me. Their maimed bodies and disfigured faces forever changed the way I feel about war.

Military conflict left many orphans in Korea, and, having lost both of my parents when I was quite young, I quickly identified with them. These children would gather around U.S. soldiers and beg for money, food, or candy. My unit adopted one of them, a little girl we called Jenny. A shy six-year-old, Jenny had a horrible scar on her neck that was certainly the result of one of the many bombings of Seoul. During my time there, she came to adopt me as her caretaker, and I did everything I could to make sure she had what she needed. I regret to this day leaving her there at the Catholic orphanage when my tour of duty was finished. A single man, I felt at the time that I had no choice.

As a result of becoming a part of Jenny's life for that short time, and seeing how war destroys people's lives, I am far more proud of the positive influence I had as a soldier than the destruction that is an inevitable result of combat. War, I now know, is a human tragedy that is only rarely necessary.

As a child, I dreamed of becoming a military leader. And as a young man, not yet 21, I joined the Army Air Corps shortly after the bombing of Pearl Harbor, determined to do my share. I always loved the military. But now as I reflect on my career, I know that it wasn't the lure of battle that drew me in, but

Introduction

rather the comradeship. I intensely wanted to *belong*.

Being a part of this cohesive group, I learned that one man working together with many can accomplish great things. With discipline, teamwork, planning, and often making do with what we're given, we can attain immense achievements. This is a theme that runs through so many of the stories in this book. And it's an idea that has carried over into my own personal philosophy.

I believe that our purpose in life is to serve. Human beings have been given so much intelligence and potential to help one another. Perhaps because I have seen so much destruction firsthand, I believe that we must try to prevent suffering by being conscious of the needs of others and taking responsibility for meeting those needs. Respecting the dignity of individuals has been an essential element of my life, and I strongly believe that all people should be treated equally and with compassion. These are not selfless actions—seeing the resulting joy in a child's face, feeling someone's pain eased, or finding solutions to what once seemed like insurmountable problems are great rewards.

This is a gift that has brought me much joy, and I hope to share it with those who read this book.

A Boy Goes to War, Arizona, 1941

CHAPTER ONE

"The Japs just bombed Pearl Harbor."

I was shaving when I heard these words, which forever changed my life. Shocked but not surprised, I was standing in front of the mirror in the community bathroom in the barracks of the Civilian Conservation Corps (CCC). After high school graduation, I had yearned for adventure. I vividly remember when Charles Lindbergh made his nonstop solo flight from New York to Paris in 1927. My mother turned to me and said, "Look at that. What have you done?" I was seven years old at the time, but it was a challenge I never forgot.

To a city boy who had grown up in the Bronx, the wide-open spaces of the West were intensely appealing. The CCC presented an opportunity to go West—to Oak Creek Canyon, near Sedona, Arizona—and to build on the engineering skills I'd acquired at Manhattan's Haaren High School engineering annex. I knew that morning in December that I would be a part of the war effort. In a way, I had been waiting for this chance to serve in the military since I was a small boy.

When my mother died, I was not yet 10. My father died when I was two. Both of my parents died of cancer. So I was sent to live with my Aunt Em, an obstetrician and pediatrician who was an assistant director for the New York Board of Health, and my Uncle John, a mechanical engineer who later worked with one of the world's top physicists, Enrico Fermi, on the Manhattan Project. Both were extremely intelligent and intellectual. Our apartment doubled as my aunt's secondary place of business, in addition to her office at the Board of Health. The apartment's second bedroom was her office. She saw patients there during the day, and at night we would set up a little cot and I slept there. My clothes were kept in a chest of drawers in the hall.

It's not too surprising that a small boy living in this intellectual atmosphere would turn to books for adventure. I voraciously read tales of King Arthur's knights, *Ivanhoe*, and Alexander Dumas' *The Three Musketeers* and all of the sequels. Later, I became entranced with flying, and read about great flying aces—Baron Manfred von Richthofen, who was Germany's Red Baron; America's Eddie Rickenbacker; General Jimmy Doolittle, famous pioneer pilot and World War II commander; Billy Bishop, a Canadian who fought for the British; and France's René Fonk.

I greatly admired German Naval Commander Count Felix von Luckner and read and reread his book *The Sea Devil*, which was filled with pictures of him in an impressive uniform. At night, on my cot in my aunt's office, I would imagine myself in his place. His ship would pose as an ordinary freighter until his target was close enough, and then the German Surface Raider would spring open hidden latches, unleashing numerous guns and taking the enemy by total surprise. What I admired most about the Count was that he always protected the British seamen and never abandoned them after sinking their ships. His interest was clearly strategic—he wanted to destroy ships, not kill innocent seamen.

My aunt, who felt my time would be better spent practicing the piano, and my uncle, who thought practicing math skills was more important, didn't understand my interests.

"Why do you read these stories," she used to ask me.

"Because I want to get away from reality," I answered, to her surprise.

Interestingly, I got to meet Count von Luckner when I was a child. I had been roller-skating in Central Park, a passion of mine along with playing hockey on skates. Flying down a narrow path, I saw too late a mother and a baby carriage coming toward me. The path wouldn't allow me to pass them, so I jumped to the side, colliding into some rocks. Lying on the grass in pain from a badly broken wrist, I didn't notice at the time the tall, husky man with a German accent who came to my aid. Later, in my aunt's office while she was setting my wrist, I realized it was Count von Luckner. He had immigrated to New York as Hitler began his rise to power.

The CCCs gave me a taste of my future in the military. Created by President Roosevelt, they were intended to help young men gain skills and ultimately find jobs. Reserve military officers acted as commanders and ran the camp. In addition, an education officer taught courses at night when we weren't working. Finally, a member of the National Park Service with the title of Project Superintendent directed projects with the help of several assistant project managers. Most of these camps were in the West. We lived in barracks while building roads, bridges, culverts, shelters, and firebreaks. It was backbreaking work, but we were young and strong. We wore green uniforms similar to those of the forest rangers, and were ranked according to positions of responsibility.

This was a tough group of kids, and I was somewhat of an outsider, having been raised by professionals in an upper middle class neighborhood. My solid high school education allowed me to quickly rise to the highest rank, which meant a raise from $30 a month to $45 a month in wages. My only income, it was a significant difference.

After working on roads and fighting fires for several months in the CCCs, I drew the attention of the Project Director. He gave me and a few other boys the job of stacking some lumber. He had given this job to some other boys first, but wasn't pleased with the results. I put myself in charge of our little crew and when we had finished, the Project Director was pleased. Soon I began to rise through the ranks, and the Project Director and I became good friends. Having always been fascinated with the military, when I had a free moment or two, I used to go into the military Commander's office and strike up a conversation to learn all I could.

These friendships proved helpful when I began to explore the possibility of going to college at the Northern Arizona State College campus nearby in Flagstaff. I visited with the college President, and because I was in the CCCs and had no money, he gave me a scholarship. The Project Superintendent made me the night watchman so that I could attend class in the daytime. My job was to stay in his office at night, and if a fire was called in, I would triangulate the location on the large map and then call various firefighting organizations. If a fire broke out while I was in class, I had to quickly leave and get back to the CCC camp to help fight the fire.

Fighting forest fires was pretty rough work. We built large firebreaks and then monitored them to make sure the fire didn't jump them. We carried 80 pounds of water in 10-gallon tanks on our backs and sprayed the breaks using hand pumps. Most nights, though, there was little activity; I could do my homework with a flashlight and sleep in a sleeping bag next to the firebreak.

Several interesting incidents happened while I was in the CCC camp that I recall as learning experiences. A Jewish Project Manager there had become the brunt of some racial jokes and challenged the aggravator to a boxing match. I heard that some of the boys planned to cut the lights when the fight began and gang up on him. With a couple of buddies, I posted myself next to the light switch and told the boys that this was going to be a fair fight. We didn't budge, and they didn't challenge us. The Project Manager won in one round.

On another occasion, several ringleaders got a group of

CCC boys to refuse to go to work, insisting on better food. As the night watchman, I observed the incident from the front door of the office. The Project Superintendent ordered the CCC group into a two-and-a-half-ton truck to be taken to the work site. They refused. He lined them up. There were only about 30 of them because the others had left for work. He ordered them several times to load up, then the camp Commander, a Captain, did the same, warning them that if they didn't, all would be dishonorably discharged. There was no response.

Then the Commander did something that I will always remember. He had the ringleader step forward. "Are you getting in the truck?" he asked.

"No," the boy replied.

"You are discharged and will be sent home," the Commander said. He then turned to another boy. "Step forward," he said.

By this time, the solid group began to melt. The Commander was taking them one at a time. Each was now separately involved and on his own to make a decision. The second boy was asked, "Are you getting in the truck?"

"Yes, sir," he said, and the strike was settled.

Another incident involved a group of boys picking on a smaller boy I liked. One morning before I left for school, the smaller boy ran into the office and told me a gang of boys had threatened him unless he resigned and left camp. He came to me for help. About this time, the gang was at the steps of the office. I knew the ringleader, who really was not too tough but liked to appear that way. I challenged him to fight me one on one. After a lengthy argument back and forth, he backed down and the incident blew over.

By the time of the attack on Pearl Harbor, I was near the end of my third full semester at college. I had left the CCC camp the summer before, attending class full time until my money ran out, and I had to go back to the CCCs in the fall. While going to summer school full time, though, I lived in the dorm. My roommate was a fellow named Paul Pertit, a Big Man on Campus who I think had become unpopular with the student body because of his close association with the faculty. Late in the spring, before we roomed together, some students broke into his room at night and shaved his head.

During the summer, there was a rumor that it was going to happen again. About that time, I was assigned as his roommate. Coming from the CCCs and having earned a reputation as a competent boxer—I was actually coaching the boxing team by this time since I didn't really have time to compete—the school assigned me as Paul's roommate. I let word get around that if anyone tried to shave Paul's head again, they would face me first and it would be one tough fight. After that, we had a quiet summer.

Although the United States did not go to war against Japan until the day after Pearl Harbor, December 8, 1941, tensions between the two nations had been mounting for several years. Japan had been aggressively expanding its borders in Asia since the late 1930s and had signed the Axis alliance with Germany and Italy. Japan's war with China had escalated to the point of intolerance by the United States. Japan had occupied Indochina, France's colony in Southeast Asia in June 1941, and since Germany occupied France, it could do nothing to defend the islands. As a consequence of those two actions, the United States, Great Britain, and Holland placed an embargo on Japan. All trade between Japan and the United States stopped completely on July 27, 1941, when President Roosevelt issued an executive order freezing all Japanese assets in the United States.

The line was drawn. These actions denied Japan the critical raw materials its industry and military needed. Japan viewed this as an unacceptable action and was working through diplomatic circles to change the mandate. In a classic misdirection play, the Japanese ambassador relayed a reply to peace discussions to the U.S. Secretary of State an hour after the bombing of Pearl Harbor had begun.

The Japanese sneak attack on the morning of December 7, 1941, severely crippled the United States' Pacific fleet and much of its air support. Three waves of Japanese planes destroyed three-fourths of the aircraft stationed at Pearl Harbor and damaged all eight battleships there. The *Arizona* was sunk and the *Oklahoma* capsized. American casualties were more than 2,300. This attack unified the American public behind the war effort, and as a young college student, I was no exception.

It is interesting to note that the American carriers, later recognized as more important than battleships, were out to sea and not harmed. The Japanese also made the mistake of attacking on a Sunday, when most of the sailors were on shore leave, reducing materially the number of trained seaman casualties. The carriers survived to fight the Battle of Midway, and experienced seaman were the nucleus of an expanded Navy.

From the moment I heard about Pearl Harbor, I was determined to join the Army Air Corps—the Air Force did not become a separate service until 1947. Since the attack had come near the end of the semester, the President of the college gave permission for all students who wanted to enlist to receive full credit for the semester even if they left early. I was one of the first to volunteer.

A few days after the attack, the head of the English Department confronted me as I walked through the halls.

"Why aren't you in class?" she asked.

"I've signed up for the Army Air Corps," was my response.

"You should be in class," came her pointed reply. "You should be in class until you leave."

Although I respected her, it was impossible for me to relate to her concern about attending class. We were at war for god sakes, and it seemed as if she just didn't get it.

I desperately wanted to enlist in the Army Air Corps as an Aviation Cadet. But even though I had attended two summer sessions, I was still six semester hours short of the two full years required to qualify. I thought briefly about sticking it out for another semester, but, even before Pearl Harbor, I had taken the physical for the draft. I was 1-A, and knew it would only be a matter of time before I was drafted—probably before I could complete the spring semester.

The recruiters for Army Air Corps arrived on campus late in December. No matter what I said, I couldn't convince them to give me a waiver to enter flight school. My love of flying had only grown since childhood. In my third year of high school, I had built an aircraft wing, meticulously designing it point by point. Each rib had to have its own separate mathematical formula. I was extremely proud of it and gave it to my Aunt Em. I'm not sure she ever understood how important that gift was to me.

The high school assigned me to Flushing Airport for practical experience. There I reported to the mechanic who maintained big-band favorite Harry Richmond's plane. Going up in that prop plane was my first experience with flight. But I had no transportation, and Flushing wasn't near a subway line. To get there I had to walk a long way, so I asked for a new assignment nearer a subway line. I was reassigned to the Navy Reserve Pilot Flight School at Floyd Bennet Field on Long Island. There I got to see the military aviators in action, which solidified my desire to do the same some day.

Finally, after yet another discussion with the recruiters regarding flight school, I remembered I had completed two evening courses at the City College of New York (CCNY) prior to entering the CCC.

"If that's true, you have your two years," the recruiter told me. "But we'll have to see the official transcripts first." I sent away for the CCNY transcripts, which arrived early in January. After reviewing the transcripts, the recruiters agreed to combine the courses together with my education at Northern Arizona State to give me credit for two years of college. By January 1942, I was off to the Army Air Corps.

I did have another offer. A university professor's husband was a recruiter for the defense aircraft industry in California and was looking for anyone with prior technical experience. Since I had an engineering background, I was offered a high salary and a draft exemption. Despite its enticing appeal, I turned down the offer. I wanted to be involved in a part of the war where I could directly make a difference.

Meanwhile, the war in the Pacific continued, badly for the Allies. A series of Japanese offensives were carefully timed to follow the attack on Pearl Harbor, and the countries and islands in the western and southwestern South Pacific suffered. Shortly after our Pacific fleet was almost destroyed, the British battleship *Prince of Wales* and the cruiser *Repulse* were sunk. With no forces to oppose them, the Japanese rapidly expanded across the Pacific. Guam and Wake Island were captured in December, and the Japanese eventually took the Philippines, Hong Kong, most of the Solomon Islands, much of northeastern New Guinea, and the Dutch East Indies. Even Australia was threatened. Bataan fell in April 1942, and Corregidor in May 1942. These first six months after we declared war were the height of glory for Japanese aggression.

At the battle for Coral Sea near Australia in May 1942, the Japanese invasion force was finally halted and forced to return to base. Our defense was costly—our carrier *Lexington* was sunk and the *Yorktown* was damaged. A month later, on June 4, 1942, another Japanese invasion force targeting Midway was defeated in the famous Battle of Midway. This battle was a total defeat for the Japanese. They lost four of their finest carriers, while we lost the *Yorktown*. This was the turning point in the Pacific war.

Meanwhile, training took me to Sheppard Air Force Base in Wichita Falls, Texas. As soon as our feet hit the ground, we began to take a variety of tests. My engineering background indicated an aptitude for mechanics, something I didn't think I was especially good at. But behind the scenes support was not what I had in mind. I wanted to go overseas and longed to be an active participant in the war effort.

It was now late 1942 and MacArthur, who was based in

Australia, was complaining that he needed people and he needed them now. The Army took everyone they could find who had completed their training and sent them to Australia. I had been scheduled for additional training, but instead was one of many young men assigned to MacArthur's Southwest Pacific theater.

I had, of course, heard of the events transpiring in the Pacific. Remote places with exotic names were now part of the newsreels. In August, the Allies had taken the offensive by attacking Guadalcanal, a southern island in the Solomons. The Allies were beginning the long fight back. Other battles, just as fierce, were going on for possession of New Guinea. The Japanese had seized the northern coast of New Guinea early on and had landed at Salamaua and Lae by March 1942. After their defeat in the Coral Sea, the Japanese decided to attack Port Moresby by land, crossing the rugged Owen Stanley Mountains. This was their prelude to invading Australia.

On July 21, 1942, Japanese troops landed at Buna and Gona, two small towns far to the southeast of Lae. From Buna, the Kokoda jungle trail led over the mountains to Port Moresby. The entire 100 miles had to be traversed on foot since the trail was narrow and, in the lowlands, was bordered by nearly impassable jungle. The ascent to the pass was steep and direct, with few opportunities for flanking movements. Large-scale, mechanical military operations were impossible there. But Japan's stripped-down infantry forces, having fought in China and throughout the Far East since December, were ready. They encountered Australians and Americans with little if any battle experience, especially in the jungle. The few Australians that the Allies had managed to recall from the Middle East were experienced only in desert warfare.

Australia was a loyal British Commonwealth nation, and as such provided many troops for action in the Middle East. When war came to the Pacific, Australia was unprepared. It had been completely stripped of manpower. By April 1942, the Japanese had taken Singapore, all of the Dutch East Indies, the Philippines, and were now approaching Australia. The Australian troops weren't recalled from Egypt because the British couldn't afford to lose the Middle East. As a result, every man available in Australia, from World War I veterans to initial draft rejects, was called up for a desperate, last-ditch resistance. They did not expect to hold forever, just long enough for the United States to arrive.

In September, the Japanese landed at Milne Bay at the far eastern point of New Guinea. After a bloody battle, they were decisively defeated by the rugged Australian force. In fighting even more savage than that occurring simultaneously at Guadalcanal, two divisions of American and Australian troops halted the Japanese advance on September 26, 1942, and began their own advance toward Buna. By January 3, 1943, Buna fell to the advancing Allies. The 5th Air Force was there to support the Army every step of the way.

A newly commissioned Second Lieutenant, I arrived in Australia in February 1943 along with about 10,000 other soldiers. We were brought to Australia on the luxury liner *Queen Mary*. In order to avoid German subs, our journey began in Boston. The route through the Indian Ocean took four weeks. The *Queen Mary* sailed alone with-

Australia, 1943. Second Lieutenant L. William Cracken before going up North.

11

out escorts, in part because no escort could have kept up with her. She was an incredibly fast ship with the ability to outrun any submarines we may have encountered. The crossing was long and boring and crowded. One major diversion was the one movie on board, *Gunga Din*, with Cary Grant. I think I could have played Cary Grant's role word for word.

Each stateroom was jammed with bunks. We were assigned quarters alphabetically, and I bunked near a fellow named Gordon Crane. We became fast friends. Gordon was the amateur golf champion for Utah and was assigned to a front line unit up North. Occasionally, when he would come to Australia where I was stationed, we would play golf in Brisbane, usually against two Australians. Though we were just playing for fun, to the Australians it was a matter of patriotism: the Yanks versus the Aussies. I was the weakest of the four golfers, but Gordon was so good he carried us. We usually won.

Several times in Brisbane I crossed MacArthur's path. Though he was certainly egotistical, I admired him as an extremely competent General. His strategy of avoiding direct attack on Japan's fortified bases in favor of peripheral, strategic battles saved many lives.

When the *Queen Mary* finally landed in Sydney, we were all glad to get off that ship. Our group was one of the first major deployments from the United States into the Southwest Pacific. This group included flying and ground crews, as well as a large contingent of infantry and support troops. Since the Australians feared imminent invasion, we were eagerly welcomed.

The Army Air Corps contingent was assigned to an old Australian camp at Baccus Marsh. While there, we had an opportunity to socialize in this little town. Unfortunately, some of our boys got a little out of hand fresh off the boat. So the Air Corps Commander of our camp selected several officers and enlisted men to act as Military Police. I was picked as the Detachment Commander. We were not given weapons, but they did manage to scrounge up some MP armbands to wear, but that was it. We would have to control the men strictly on personality. Each detachment had 12 men, and I soon learned that facial expressions and body language can be a lot more intimidating than words.

Overall, we had no major problems in Baccus Marsh. However, later on in Brisbane, there was a more serious incident. Australians would line up to buy cigarettes at the American BX. One Aussie in line was drunk, got out of hand, and hit an MP. The MP fired at the ground to get the man to back off, but the bullet ricocheted and hit him in the chest, killing him. Australian soldiers there began to riot. It looked like it was getting worse, so my Commander recruited me and about 30 other GIs to go down there for a show of force. My GIs had carbines but no ammunition. I had my .45 with six rounds. The moment the Australians saw the truck with GIs carrying carbines, they settled down. No one got hurt.

At this time, General George Kenney, the new Commander of the 5th Air Force and Commander-in-Chief of all Allied Air Forces in the Southwest Pacific, had determined that the 4th Air Depot Group at Townsend was inadequate for the needs of his Air Force. He created another Air Depot Group in

Brisbane and designated it the 81st Air Depot Group—to complement the already existing 4th, which specialized in engines, airframe, and avionics repair. Key personnel from the 4th, along with airmen with previous mechanical backgrounds and those with high aptitude scores in mechanics, were pulled out of the camp at Baccus Marsh and assigned to the newly forming 81st group. I was not happy to be a part of this group, and would have preferred to go straight to a line unit.

The 81st was based at Eagle Farm near Brisbane. Our main charge was to reassemble crated B-25 and A-20 light bombers and the P-47 and P-38 fighters. It was too far to fly them from the United States, so they had to be disassembled, shipped over, then reassembled in Australia. Once we had them in one piece again, we would test fly them and send them north to the combat zone. We also performed major engine overhauls—disassembling engines, testing them for any cracks in the metal, and finally reassembling them and getting them back out to the front.

Before the war, Eagle Farm was a regional airstrip with a single runway used primarily for private planes and intra-Australia commercial traffic. When the Americans arrived, we greatly enhanced the runways, building hangars for maintenance, a control tower, and other buildings as required. The once sleepy field changed almost overnight into a flourishing maintenance depot and a small city of more than 3,000.

Fairly early on, a representative from the 5th Air Force came and spoke to us, asking for volunteers for a secret flying mission. I was so enthusiastic that I left the dining room where we were meeting and went over to headquarters to volunteer. I told my Commander that I wanted to be in that program. Later, when they published the list of six officers who had been selected for the mission, my name wasn't there. The Commander had forgotten to mention me to the 5th Air Force representative. I tried to be added, but was told it was too late; the orders were already out, and they did not want to take anyone off the list.

Though I knew that operational readiness was a critical aspect of successful air operations, staying behind to keep the planes in the air was initially disappointing. I was somewhat more enthused by our efforts to enhance combat performance. The balance between having enough bombs on board an aircraft and having too many is a delicate one. Too many, and you limit a plane's ability to maneuver and to fly long distances. Too few, and the raids are ineffective. One of our jobs was to find the right balance. Our maintenance crew also performed major engine overhaul on Pratt & Whitney and Wright engines for B-24 and B-17 heavy bombers. We would take the engines apart, test them, and reassemble them. Novices when we arrived, we soon became experts.

Soon after my arrival, a captured Zero "Zeke" Japanese fighter was sent to our group. We placed it in a secured hangar and tested it for flight characteristics to determine the best way to counter and defeat the fighter. Everything we learned provided a clue to the American pilots who faced the Zeke daily.

After the fall of Guadalcanal, the Japanese base at Lae became critical to the defense of New Guinea and Rabaul, a major Japanese base farther north. The Commanding General of the Japanese Armies in the Solomons and New Guinea decided to reinforce the garrison at Lae. On March 1, 1943, a convoy of eight transports and eight destroyers left Rabaul for the Bismarck Sea and Lae. As the convoy lumbered toward its destination, they were spotted, and the U.S. 5th Air Force units were responsible for stopping them in the Battle of the Bismarck Sea.

We had specially modified our bomber to allow the planes to release their bombs just before reaching the target. With a five-second delay, the planes could be safely away from the ensuing explosion. In March, these planes took to the air in the Battle of the Bismarck Sea and, using this technique, destroyed a number of Japanese troop ships and barges that were to reinforce the Japanese troops in New Guinea. This was my first contribution to major combat experience.

Occasionally, while taking a plane to Port Moresby or test-ing planes in New Guinea, my unit would encounter Japanese fighters. Our P-47 was powerful. It had tremendous climb, was extremely deadly, and far superior to the Japanese Zeke with better armor and armaments. Although the Zekes were more maneuverable, they were vulnerable to attack, having very little protection. If hit anywhere, they were goners. We knew the Zeke's weaknesses and could readily defeat the plane. Ameri-can pilots generally won by closing in, conserving their ammunition, and keeping their planes' noses pointed toward the tail of the enemy. The fighters we ferried from Eagle Farm to the front were fully combat ready, complete with loaded guns. We did not expect enemy interference, but we were pre-pared. From time to time our planes were intercepted and we had to fire in self-defense.

The American offensive continued with the invasion of New Georgia in the Solomons and advancement in New Guinea. In June 1943, the Americans landed at Nassau Bay, 60 miles south of Lae. In October, with Australian and Ameri-can infantrymen slugging up the coast toward Salamaua, an amphibious force landed on the coast north of Lae and quickly captured the strong-point. Finschafen fell on October 2, and the Huon Gulf was now Allied Territory. By December 1943, forces landed on the Southern and Western coasts of New Britain, building bases to effectively neutralize and isolate Rabaul. The Slot, as it was called, was now totally under the control of Allied forces.

The 5th Air Force, under General Kenney, earned a reputa-tion for innovative and fierce combat. Tokyo Rose, the famous Japanese radio announcer, called Kenney The Beast and his men a gang of gangsters. The 5th Air Force's bag of tricks was large and diverse. When enemy antiaircraft fire interfered with its missions, pilots dropped white phosphorus to blind Japa-nese gunners on the ground. Dummy airfields were constructed to confuse the enemy. Massive paratroop drops, including two-

and-a-half-ton trucks dropped from C-47s, were successful and commonplace.

The 5th also used the "parafrag," a small fragmentation bomb with a parachute attached to slow its descent. Bombers could fly in at treetop height, drop their bombs, and still have time to escape the explosions. Using these bombs, the 5th demolished scores of Japanese planes when bombing airstrips. By late 1943, the 5th Air Force had gained total air superiority over New Guinea.

Our Eagle Farm engineering group under Major and later Lieutenant Colonel "Pappy" Gunn played a major role in developing many tactics and weapons. Gunn was a bush pilot in the Philippines who had escaped the Japanese. He was instrumental in developing many of the new weapons the 5th Air Force used so effectively against the Japanese. Our work centered around finding the means to give B-25s more firepower to enable them to defend themselves en route to their bombing targets. Under Gunn's direction, we ripped out the bombardier's position in the nose of the plane and fit each plane with .50 caliber machine guns armed with 500 rounds of ammunition apiece. When the additional weight made the plane's nose heavy, three of the guns were removed and an extra 200-gallon gas tank was added behind the wings to correct the balance. The plane's two top turret guns were modified so they could be locked in an automatic forward-firing position.

This 10-gun plane, with four guns in the nose, two in each wing, and two up top, became the prototype for bomber strafes for the rest of the war. The results were devastating for the Japanese. Other improvements included .50 caliber pocket guns along the side and .75 millimeter cannons. Rockets were beginning to be used, and I specifically assisted in the development of procedures for using these new weapons. We also worked on improving the gun sights and the guns on the P-47s.

As MacArthur advanced in New Guinea, functions of the

81st were moved forward. General Kenney was an aggressive airman and wanted his support groups close to the front. We were reassigned to Finschafen, New Guinea, in October 1943, shortly after it was captured, to become an advance base for the front lines. Some units still remained at Eagle Farm to assemble the aircraft being shipped in from the United States. At Finschafen, we set up a mobile unit to fix the engines we could. Those requiring major repairs went to Eagle Farm.

New Guinea was my first encounter with the jungle. A long mountain range extends from the island's northwest to southeast ends, with peaks that rise to more than 16,000 feet above sea level. The coasts are swampy, and much of the interior is covered with dense rain forests thickly overgrown with tropical vegetation. Just south of the equator, New Guinea was the hottest climate I had ever experienced. Daily rainfall brought humidity and mosquitoes. Technically, we were always out of uniform, rarely wearing a thing from the waist up to survive the heat. I'm still extremely particular about the water I drink after the months of forcing down barely potable water in New Guinea, which was dispensed from large rubber bags. In our tents at night, we could hear the crabs scratching on the canvas as they made their way up and over in a continuous migration from the sea.

Our work meant a lot to General Kenney. An unassuming fellow, he used to come to the field and watch the technical developments in process. Kenney was people conscious and wanted to protect "his boys," no matter the cost. He wanted to give them all the advantages he could while they were in the air. As with any war, we lost pilots; to the General, every one of them was a name, not just a number. He wanted to win, but he wanted to win as efficiently as possible, minimizing his own casualties. Many years later, General Kenney wrote a pilot program for television about two 5th Air Force pilots and their mechanic. During the war, my nickname was Crack, and he named the mechanic in his show Crack. The program was only aired twice that I'm aware of. I contacted NBC, ABC, and CBS, but none had a copy.

By this time in the war, the Japanese had lost most of their good pilots, but they still had considerable capability. Now forced to resupply isolated bases with fast barges, the Air Force began to search for the supply routes, sinking those ships whenever possible. With this nuance, our role changed again as we began to develop weapons to assist in the interdiction efforts. Some of these projects included installing a .75 millimeter cannon on the B-25s to make them much more dangerous to the ships, as well as .50 caliber machine guns and .20 millimeter cannons and pocket guns on either side of the B-25.

Though my work was interesting and I knew we were aiding the war effort, I still had the desire to get into a tactical unit and become involved in the real fighting. I was particularly fascinated with reconnaissance. Recon flights were not for the faint-of-heart. These planes would fly alone against high-value, heavily defended targets, generally deep into enemy territory. They would go over the target early, before the main raid, or they would fly in after the raid for bomb damage assessment. They had to fly straight over the target to take photographs. The enemy knew they were coming and what they were there for, and would aim every gun at the usually solo reconnaissance plane. The loss rate was generally higher for these flights than for either strike bombers or fighter escorts. Experienced pilots were generally assigned. I would have to wait for another war, Korea, to get involved in this effort.

Whenever I got the chance with General Kenney, I would ask for an assignment in a more active area. Invariably, the General would say, "Crack, we need you here." I was not the only one to ask for front-line assignments. General Kenney must have gotten tired of saying no.

On January 2, 1944, the Americans took Saidor and its airfield. To the east, in April 1944, MacArthur captured the Admiralty Islands, thus surrounding Rabaul and providing an important advance base and port. Also in April, he bypassed the heavily held Japanese positions on Wewak in order to land on Hollandia, an important harbor and eventually the destination for more than 30,000 U.S. troops. Simultaneously, Aitape was secured with its airfield. In late May 1944, MacArthur sent the 41st Division to Biak, a small island on the far western coast of New Guinea that had three airfields. The 5th Air Force provided the necessary cover for every mile. I visited Biak Island. The water was like syrup due to its volcanic base, and the crabs were everywhere.

On September 15, 1944, MacArthur's troops landed unopposed on Morotai. The Japanese had concentrated their efforts on the nearby Halmahera Islands, believing Morotai incapable of supporting an air base. Halmahera was base for 30,000 Japanese troops. Despite swamps, the Americans constructed two airfields, one for bombers and one for fighters, and began using them in early October to attack the Balikpapan refineries and Mindanao, as well as to support the Leyte landings. From Morotai, our air forces played a major role in supporting the Philippines invasion and attacked Dutch East Indies bases to the west.

The 13th Air Force was originally assigned to the Navy and stationed at Manus, in the Admiralty Islands. But MacArthur asked the Joint Chiefs of Staff to assign the 13th Air Force to him. They agreed. General Kenney took over command of the 13th as well as the 5th Air Force and became the Commander-in-Chief of the Far East Air Forces. When he took over the 13th Air Force, it was undermanned and somewhat ineffective, having limited maintenance capabilities. The General started looking for people, those he knew and could trust, especially those from his other command, the 5th Air Force.

Though my tour was up and I could have gone home, General Kenney asked me to reconsider and join his new command.

I never gave it a second thought. "I'll go," I told him, and began my second tour in the Pacific.

Keeping Our Boys in the Air, South Pacific, 1944-1945

Chapter Two

One of General Kenney's first orders for the 13th was to move the two heavy bombing wings, the 307th and the 5th, to Morotai. So in October 1944, I was off to Morotai to assist the Director of Maintenance for the 13th Bomber Command.

These heavy bombers, B-24s, were flying missions from Morotai to Borneo, the Philippines, Celebes, and the Moluccas. General William Matheny was our commander, affectionately nicknamed WAM, since his full name was William A. Matheny. "WAM" was appropriate for his spirited, action-oriented style. He had three B-24 command planes used for logistics, inspections, and command missions. These were specifically my responsibility.

I flew with the bomber command Staff Maintenance Officer, but not on combat missions. However, we flew with full crews and armament in case we were intercepted. I helped test the planes for cruise control, weight and balance, fuel distribution, bomb loading, and fuel allocations to increase the range of the bombing missions from Morotai. On one mission, the command plane, with 10 passengers aboard—including the Chief-of-Staff of the 13th Air Force Bomber Command, Colonel Stevens—took off on a scheduled flight to the Admiralties. I missed this flight because my wisdom teeth hurt so badly that I had to make a trip to the infirmary to have them pulled. The plane probably experienced radio problems and thus was not able to give its location when it went down somewhere in the thousand miles of ocean between Morotai and Manus islands. No sign of the plane was ever found.

Typically during bombing missions, PBYs (which we called Dumbos), submarines, or small ships were assigned as rescue vehicles near the target or on the line of flight to the target to pick up any downed airmen. Unfortunately, no rescue vehicles were assigned or nearby this routine flight. If it weren't for the hospital stay, I would have been on that plane.

Morotai is a small island just north of the Halmaheras, which were Japanese territory. Though we were in extremely close proximity to the enemy, it seemed like the Japanese and the Americans had an informal understanding to avoid each other. The Japanese knew that if they attacked, they probably would be wiped out by our overwhelming air power and the U.S. ground forces protecting us on the island. The Americans knew that if we attacked, many people would be killed with little to show for the gain. Another factor in the apparent truce was that both sides knew the war was winding down. So the attitude was, why fight and die for terrain that didn't matter and wouldn't influence the war's end result? When we took off from Morotai, we would often fly directly over the Japanese, but they rarely if ever shot at us.

Though we worked around the clock and every day of the week, Morotai was a beautiful island with gorgeous shoreline and a beach made for resort living. We enjoyed ourselves when we could, sitting out on the beach and watching the waves come in at sunset. Sometimes it was difficult to believe that we were in the middle of the war. Then, at night, we would look out over the dark ocean and see flashes of light in the darkened sky. The flashes were from naval actions between American PT-boats and the Japanese barges attempting to resupply their garrisons.

We did have our share of close encounters. We had a number of red alerts signaling air attacks. During these we took cover in our self-built air raid shelters or away from the buildings that were likely targets. One bomb hit the base post office, and we were without mail for a while. The air raids were so numerous, we got strangely comfortable with them. Sometimes I even stayed in my bunk under my mosquito net sound asleep and learned of a raid the following morning. Typically, our runways were the primary target for these Japanese bombers, who were usually from Japanese air bases such as Truk and Rabaul.

We came to call the Japanese Bedtime Charlies. Once, late at night, a Sergeant and I were in a jeep heading to the airfield to check one of the planes for an early morning mission. I looked up and saw a Japanese Betty, a bomber, flying right over us. All I can say is that the Japanese must not have thought we were valuable enough to warrant a bomb. Perhaps the fact that our headlights were dimmed saved us.

Once a black alert was predicted—meaning a land invasion was imminent. We took that warning very seriously. I had been assigned to assist in the design of pillboxes and defensive positions around the headquarters of the 13th Bomber Command. Though an Army division was assigned to Morotai, we weren't sure its numbers were adequate for defense of the island in the case of invasion. We prepared to defend our headquarters, but thankfully, the invasion never materialized.

Several times, Tokyo Rose falsely broadcast the message that the Japanese army had reoccupied Morotai. She did so on Christmas in 1944, while we were safe and alive.

Though the Japanese threat was real, we didn't consciously focus on it. We did, however, joke about the dangers of life on a tropical island. From the time I arrived in New Guinea until I left Morotai, I always slept under mosquito nets. It was automatic, you didn't think twice about it. If you didn't use the nets, you would be eaten alive by mosquitoes. The standard joke at the time was, "While I was sleeping I heard two mosquitoes talking to each other about me. One said, 'Shall we eat him here or take him back home and eat him?' The other said, 'Let's eat him here. If we take him home, the big boys will eat him.'" When I got stateside, it took me a while to get used to sleeping without the nets.

Tropical disease was always a health threat. Every morning we had to take our Atabrine, an antimalarial drug. Quinine, the typical antimalarial drug, was not available to us since some of its ingredients came from the Dutch East Indies—which were occupied by the Japanese. Atabrine had an unusual side effect—it turned the skin yellow. But the unusual complexion turned out to be an asset in dating. Australian girls could tell if a soldier had been in the jungle by the color of his skin. If you weren't tinted yellow, then you had not yet been up North, a trip the girls considered heroic and exotic.

While in Brisbane, I met a number of Australian girls, but there was one in particular I really liked—Fay. We maintained a relationship even after I was assigned to New Guinea and Morotai. I tried to fly to Australia to see her as often as I could, and luckily this could be managed in conjunction with my official duties. An important part of general maintenance was to optimize fuel consumption through correct weight and balance. Townsend, back in Australia, had a large scale for aircraft. My unit often had to fly to Townsend where the 4th Air Depot was located. Once in Australia, we would hop a C-47 flight over to Brisbane to see the girls.

In Brisbane, I got to know a former professional boxer who was running a gym. I used to work out with him, and he learned that I had done some boxing and had coached the team at Northern Arizona State. One time when I came down from New Guinea on leave, he introduced me to the editor of the Brisbane newspaper, who was an amateur boxer. My friend suggested a sparring contest. I had a touch of malaria at the time, but I obliged. It turned out to be very embarrassing. The newspaper editor was a much more proficient boxer. We went three rounds, and I lost every one.

As the war progressed in 1945, one by one the islands of the Philippines were invaded. The Americans made progress, and by March 1945, General Matheny told me, "Cracken, you've been here long enough. It's time to go home."

The war was nearing its end. A point system had been created that was based upon overseas duty and decorations. According to that system, I had more points than most of the others. I didn't want to leave Morotai and told the General I was in no hurry to go.

"You're going back," General Matheny told me. "I've been looking at your record. You've got enough points here. I'd look bad if I didn't send you home." Commanders were criticized for keeping men in combat beyond a normal tour of duty.

So, after successfully pulling two tours in the South Pacific over two years, I returned to the U.S. in the spring of 1945 as a First Lieutenant. My first stop stateside was the Santa Ana Air Base near Los Angeles, a rest camp for returning airmen. There were two camps in the area—Long Beach Air Base for married officers and Santa Ana for bachelors. The camps were for decompression, a place for returning airmen to get out of the war mode before being reassigned to stateside duty. We were all interviewed to help the Air Force determine our next assignment.

With the war still on, Los Angeles had two officers' clubs, one in each of two prestigious downtown hotels. The girls that were hostesses in the clubs came from the best families in Los Angeles. Being a hostess was considered a glamorous duty, and there was a waiting list for girls who wanted to volunteer. At this time, soldiers were still being sent overseas. Only a few were returning. Anyone with a medal or ribbon received special attention from both the girls and the civilians. Civilians bought us drinks, and the girls literally hovered over us. Without a ribbon, you were just another back home guy; with a ribbon you became someone special.

During my short time at the rest camp, I dated several young ladies in Los Angeles. One girl came from a very prominent family. She wanted me to meet her parents, but I was reluctant to get involved. Having been raised by my aunt and uncle after my own parents died, I had never known a loving family life. I always had doubts about getting serious and thought I would never make a good husband and father. Another girl, the one I preferred, was the piano player at the officers' club, but there wasn't enough time for us to get close.

The most famous nightspot at the time was the Hollywood Canteen. It was for enlisted men only, so I wasn't supposed to enter. However, I learned you could get in the back door and take a stairway to the second floor where you could look down on the activity. Once I decided to drop by and check out the popular scene. I remember it was raining, and I was wearing a raincoat that showed my rank but covered my ribbons. Since most of the officers were going overseas and not coming back, it was natural for people to presume I was waiting to go rather than returning from two tours. Sonny Tufts, a local Hollywood celebrity at the time, was one of the entertainers that evening at the Hollywood Canteen. Sonny spotted me as I entered the club and told me it was only for enlisted men.

"I understand there is a place upstairs where officers can go to watch," I said, beginning to make my way there.

"Well, if you want to go around the back, yes," he replied in an indifferent tone.

I went upstairs and took off my raincoat. When I came back downstairs, I didn't think about it, but all of my overseas ribbons were visible. Sonny looked at me and realized that I had just returned from overseas. He immediately became friendly and attentive. Soldiers who returned from the war were treated with exceptional courtesy and politeness, particularly if they were decorated. Sonny was self-conscious about not being in the service, and when he saw all of my ribbons, he was uncomfortable. He tried hard that night to compensate for his earlier attitude.

One weekend shortly thereafter, I was asleep in my hotel room in Los Angeles. On weekends we were allowed to leave the base. My door was unlocked, which was pretty normal practice at the time. I heard some noise and woke up to find a young man in a Marine uniform standing over me. Instantly I reacted. I threw my blanket over him and pushed him down. The Marine hit his head against the wall and slumped to the ground just as I noticed a second man in a Marine uniform standing over by the closet. That's where I'd put my clothes and money—considerable back pay that was due from my overseas duty when I arrived stateside. I pushed the second man against the wall, and the two didn't make a move while I called the house detective. He came up right away and took the two burglars to the police.

As it turned out, they weren't real Marines, but had stolen Marine uniforms. They were going from room to room looking for an unlocked door. Back in camp later that week, I got a call from the police asking me to come over in a couple of weeks to testify against them. I really didn't want to testify and had a good excuse. "I'll be gone," I told the detective.

The very next night, I was back in my room at camp and

woke to see a man in uniform looking at me. He was some distance away, and I didn't feel quite as lucky as on the previous night. I just froze. So did the man. When I finally moved, I discovered that the man standing there wasn't a man at all—it was my uniform hanging on the closet door.

One of the more interesting activities for returning officers was attending Masquers Club meetings. The Hollywood movie producers at the time had a private club called the Masquers Club. They met every two weeks to discuss various matters concerning production problems in Hollywood. During the war, the club asked the Red Cross office at the base to select six returning bachelor officers to attend their dinner meeting as guests of the club. I guess they viewed this as their contribution to the war effort. Before dinner, the producers would introduce the officers to single starlets who were the escorts for the evening. After dinner, the starlets showed the officers around Hollywood and usually went dancing.

As soon as I heard about it, I went to the camp's Red Cross Office to sign up for the next outing. The night I attended, my host was the producer Mervyn LeRoy. Sitting on the other side of Mr. LeRoy was Marilyn Maxwell, a minor starlet and my date. She was great looking but not my type. She spent an inordinate amount of time talking about herself. At the time, I had a big crush on Olivia De Havilland. During dinner, I said aside to Mr. LeRoy, "I've always admired Olivia De Havilland. Do you think there might be an opportunity for me to meet her. I understand she's not married."

"Well, I'll look into it and let you know," he said. "She may not be available, but if you'll attend the next meeting, I'll see."

The next day I went to the Red Cross Office and asked for the clipboard to sign up for the Masquers Club.

"That's two weeks from now," the Red Cross girl told me. "We don't put the sign-in sheet out until a day or two before the meeting."

"I want to be sure I'm on that list," I said.

Every day I walked over to the Red Cross Office and

checked for the sign-in clipboard. A few days before the next meeting, I was in the mess hall eating when a friend came up to me and told me that President Roosevelt had just died. I was truly saddened about the President's death because I thought he was a great leader. But later in the day I learned of the personal cost to me. When I walked to the Red Cross Office for my daily ritual of checking on the Masquers Club list, I noticed the door to the Red Cross Office was closed. A notice on the door read, "Closed for one month in honor of President Roosevelt's death." By the time the month was up and the office reopened, I would be long gone. I never got the chance for my dream date.

Santa Ana had a nice tennis facility, and a friend and I used to play. One day the tennis coach for the base stopped to watch us. Soon another officer came by who recognized the coach as former World Amateur Tennis Champion Fred Perry of England. I stopped playing and asked Sergeant Perry if he wouldn't mind hitting the ball with me and giving me some tips. He kindly obliged. Some years later in Maryland, I met him again. We were both in the Salisbury television station for separate interviews, and I made the mistake of telling the station manager that I knew Fred Perry. To my embarrassment, and Perry's, the manager called him over, pointing me out as an old friend. I should have just kept quiet.

We were permitted to leave the base on weekends, so I took a short trip back to Northern Arizona State. I had a nice time and was able to have dinner with one of my former professors. I also wanted to pick up some of my belongings that I had left there. When I headed out for the war, I put everything I valued into a small footlocker and left it with the school custodian in the basement. When I returned, the basement had been remodeled for the ROTC unit, and my footlocker was long gone.

In April 1945, shortly before VE day, I was assigned to Eglin Air Force Base in Florida, the proving ground for the now Army Air Forces. I was assigned to a project that dealt with the first air missile program using the JB-2. The JB-2 was an almost perfect copy of the German V-1 missile. The factories that produced them actually used German blueprints. In those days just prior to and immediately after the end of fighting in Europe, a top priority mission was for us to test the JB-2 missiles for use in the invasion of Japan. Our specific goal was to test them for launching from an American Landing Ship Tank, LST, off the shore of Japan.

The Germans launched the V-1s from a 40-foot ramp and used hydrogen peroxide as a propellant. The original V-1 continued until its fuel was exhausted, then it fell from the sky and exploded upon impact. This was a rudimentary guidance system. The Germans really had no way to determine when and where the missiles would come down. Since they were aiming for London, they had a large target that was tough to miss. The V-1 was vulnerable since it flew just slightly slower than Allied fighters did. If a fighter could intercept a missile in mid-flight and get behind it, the fighter could easily destroy the missile. Though many were destroyed in this way, many others found their targets, causing severe damage to the British capital.

At Eglin Field, we made several modifications. First and foremost was creating a better guidance system. Our special project team was specifically asked to design a different launching system. Forty-foot ramps on LSTs were infeasible. There was just not enough room. We had to design a zero-launch ramp—meaning a ramp the length of the missile itself. We were also asked to experiment with different propellants. Hydrogen peroxide was too volatile. The resulting fumes could cause an explosion or overpower anyone near the missile. The propellant we chose was steam. We were ahead of our time. Steam later became the primary propellant for catapults to launch planes from American Navy Carriers.

Our testing ground was on Santa Rosa Island, a remote island off the coast of Florida. We launched the missiles into the Gulf of Mexico. While we took our work seriously, we were also somewhat of a sideshow for many VIPs visiting Eglin who wanted to see some action. It was not unusual for a senator or congressman to be on hand to watch us launch these missiles into the Gulf. We flew an escort, generally using P-51 fighters, for each missile. If a missile varied from the predetermined track, we blew it up over the Gulf.

In May, the Army began a gradual demobilization according to the point system based on overseas time and decorations. With one of the highest point totals at Eglin Field, I could have left the service at any time during my stay there. I still had a desire to complete my college education, so I applied to and was accepted at Columbia University in New York, where my Uncle John Viscardi had graduated with honors in engineering.

On a quick visit after the war to see my Aunt Em and Uncle John, I noticed that a New York newspaper actually had want ads begging for returning vets on its front page. Companies were desperate for good help with so many men still at war. I was tempted to leave the Air Force and apply for one of those jobs. But just before I was to leave for Columbia to continue my studies, I read a Base Bulletin indicating the Army needed military government officers for Germany very badly. They wanted men with engineering backgrounds, particularly civil engineers. Even though my education was in a different field, my general engineering background was sufficient to qualify.

I was entranced with the possibility. After being in the steamy jungles of the South Pacific for over two years, I was intrigued with going to Europe. I had long been a student of European history and wanted to see it in person prior to going back to college. I knew I could always go to college. This was a once-in-a-lifetime opportunity, so I applied for the military government school and was accepted.

Soon after I submitted my application, the Base Commander, Colonel Hubert Zemke, one of the leading fighter aces in Europe and a former prisoner of war, called me in.

The Colonel had had his fill of Europe and asked me why I wanted to go. "You have enough points to get out of the service. Why don't you just get out and go to Columbia and finish your schooling?"

The Colonel was trying to provide guidance to a young man, much like I would try to do for others 20 years later. But I was not dissuaded. I was young and wanted to see Europe.

The military government school was at the University of Virginia in Charlottesville. It was a three-month course for students to train in all aspects of municipal government, from management to control of utilities and finances. I bought a car from a friend at Eglin and started on my way. The car broke down halfway there, near Tuskegee, Alabama. It would have cost more to fix than it was worth, so I sold the car as junk to a local car dealer and continued the journey on bus.

When I finally got to Virginia, it was December 1945. I reported to the Queen Charlotte Hotel, where the students were quartered. The hotel manager gave me a room at the very front of the hotel. It was freezing, especially to me, having come from sunny Florida. I immediately went back to tell the manager that my radiator wasn't working.

"We'll fix it," he told me. Three months later, when I was getting ready to depart for my new assignment, it still had not been fixed. A year later, I returned to Charlottesville to visit old friends, and the manager gave me the same room.

"Does it have heat?" I asked.

"No, but we'll fix it. It's the best room we have," was his pat reply.

"I was here last year, and it didn't have heat then," I said.

"To tell the truth," the manager finally admitted, "we can't fix it. The boiler is an old one, and it doesn't have enough pressure to force heat to that front room."

He finally gave me a new room, the least he could do after having made me sleep under two blankets through the prior winter.

At Charlottesville, I was joined by about 30 classmates

and, in addition to the cold room, was greeted with bad news. Apparently they now had plenty of military government officers in Europe. However, an acute shortage had been noted elsewhere. My class was not going to Germany. Instead, we were going halfway across the globe in the other direction—to Korea.

Discovering Pusan, Korea, 1946-1947

CHAPTER THREE

I returned to the Pacific in the spring of 1946 on a troop ship filled with replacements for one of the divisions in Korea. I think it was the 1st Cavalry Division. With 5,000 soldiers on board, enlisted men slept in hammocks hung in three and four tiers. As an officer, a Lieutenant, I had quarters, but they still managed to jam several of us into each stateroom built for two. It was cramped but smooth sailing, and no one suffered during the trip from California.

I didn't ship out with my graduating class from the military government school because I came down with a case of the mumps. Awaiting debarkation in San Francisco, I went out with a friend for a big night on the town. We met two pretty girls at the St. Francis Hotel before I started feeling badly. Back at the base, I found out I had the mumps. Still, I didn't miss out on romance completely. While I was in quarantine and waiting for the next ship to Korea, I met a nurse named Dorothy. We were a hot item for those few weeks, and corresponded during the early part of my time in Korea.

The United States was not prepared to occupy Korea. The

military had planned from the beginning to occupy Europe and had organized courses to train military governors to be ready when the time came. But at the end of the war, based on the political agreement between the Allies, the U.S. Army occupied South Korea and the Soviet Army occupied North Korea. By late fall of 1945, the need for trained military governors in Korea was acute. Having sufficient units in Europe, the next military government class from the University of Virginia, which just happened to be the one I was in, was sent to Korea.

Before arriving in Korea, my military government classmates and I learned various aspects of the Korean culture and language. This was the first and only class taught specifically for Korea. One of our instructors was a retired Presbyterian missionary. He taught us enough of the language to get ourselves in trouble, and, later, I would find my Korean interpreter, Kim, invaluable to my daily work.

As occupation of Korea was truly an afterthought, little information was readily available to us to study. Our other instructors were expert civil engineers and those trained in municipal operations. The emphasis of the class was to become municipal officers—to run a city like Seoul or Pusan just as a mayor or city manager would.

Korea had been called a dagger pointed at the heart of Japan. For a millennium, it had served as the direct route for Chinese invasions of Japan as well as Japan's retaliations and advances on China. The Japanese victory in the Russo-Japanese War (1904-1905) led to the formal Japanese annexation of Korea in 1910. Japan assumed total control and began efforts aimed at assimilation, including such extreme measures as the outlawing of the Korean language and even of Korean family names. These practices stopped only with the defeat of Japan in World War II, and resulted in a people beaten down by more than a half-century of oppression and discrimination.

In 1943, Roosevelt, Churchill, and Chiang Kai-Shek resolved in the Cairo Declaration to liberate Korea. However, at the Yalta Conference in 1945, Roosevelt said it would take 20 to 30 years before Korea was ready for complete independence. Yalta called for a Soviet declaration of war on Japan within 90 days of victory in Europe. Shortly before the end of the war in the Pacific, the U.S.S.R. invaded Manchuria and Korea, easily pushing aside any token Japanese forces before them. Belatedly, it was determined that Soviet entry into the Pacific effort was probably not necessary.

Still, at Yalta, the U.S. and the U.S.S.R. had divided Korea at the 38th parallel for the purpose of accepting the surrender of Japanese troops. Surprisingly, despite Western fears and no nearby Allied units, after the surrender, Soviet troops south of the parallel did return to the North.

The 38th parallel was an arbitrary artificial boundary with no natural features. South Korea and North Korea combined are 86,000 square miles, just slightly larger than Utah. The American zone, South Korea, contained about 42 percent of

the land and two-thirds of the estimated 30 million Korean population. This area was primarily agricultural and served traditionally as the breadbasket to the North. The Soviet zone was rich in mineral deposits and manufacturing facilities. It contained several hydroelectric plants that were considered at the time among the best in the world.

The first American troops, units of the XXIV Corps, landed at Korea's Port of Inchon on September 8, 1945. The XXIV Corps commander, Lieutenant General John Hodge, was the overall military commander in Korea until 1949, when the last of the American troops were evacuated. Since the Koreans had not governed themselves for over 50 years, Americans believed we had to come in, take over the government, and teach them how to run it. Most of the prewar civil servants were Japanese, and Korean management talent was lacking immediately postwar, when the Japanese were forced back to Japan. For most every American government official, there was, or were plans for, a Korean counterpart. We soon found that some Koreans were as well-trained as we were and knew more about the Korean problems and how to solve them than their assigned American mentors.

After my arrival in Japan, I flew over to Seoul. There had been no major bombings in Seoul during World War II, but it still immediately struck me as a very sad city. The buildings were far from modern and were run-down and dingy. People crowded the streets trying to stay out of the way of Americans rumbling through the city in two-and-a-half-ton trucks. My first night in Korea was spent on a cot in the ballroom of a hotel that had been set up for the many American servicemen who were there to get the country running again.

The morning after my arrival in Seoul, I walked outside of the hotel to catch the next truck headed for military headquarters where I would get my assignment. I quickly learned that I was headed south to the Port of Pusan, having been assigned to the Department of Transportation.

The military government of Korea was very similar to the

British Colonial offices of the 19th and early 20th centuries. I've always admired the British and how they managed their empire. Growing up, one of my favorite movies was *Sanders of the River*, which vividly depicted the sacrifices and dedication of the British Colonial government. During the height of the British Empire, many district officers under the Colonial Ministry in London positively influenced large numbers of colonial subjects in their management. The military government officers in Korea faced challenges that can be likened to the British in Africa and India, where a mere handful of well-trained colonial officers ran entire countries. Like them, we easily could have been overrun by the multitudes we governed if we did our jobs poorly. And we had the added threat of the Soviets to the North always trying to undermine us. Unlike the British or the Soviets in North Korea, though, the American military government did not view its position in South Korea as permanent. Our charge was to enable the South Koreans to become self-governing.

The military government team consisted of a group of departments. The federal departments operated the national agencies; the municipal departments operated the provinces and cities. The Department of Transportation consisted of three bureaus—the Highway Bureau, the Railroad Bureau, and the Marine Bureau. I was assigned to the Marine Bureau, and though it was headquartered in Seoul, I was sent to Pusan to the Port Authority there to serve as the Executive Officer and Port Engineer. In Seoul, I reported to the Chief of the Marine Bureau, Lieutenant Colonel Nelson, and ultimately to the head of the Department of Transportation, Colonel Carnelson.

When Lieutenant Colonel Nelson gave me my assignment, he was immediately apologetic. He felt Pusan was not a particularly good assignment. He had never been down there, thought it was too remote, and had heard that the food wasn't so great. In Seoul, the officers lived in a decent hotel, the Officers' Club was far superior to the one in Pusan, and, in general, there was more to do. But he explained that an officer with engineering experience was desperately needed. He promised that as soon as possible, he would get me transferred back to Seoul.

Given that buildup, it was with some trepidation that I set out for Pusan. The major connection between Seoul and Pusan was an old, rickety train that occasionally got shot up by Korean bandits and communist infiltrators. A C-47 that belonged to the municipal government was sometimes available, and I got lucky and was given a lift down. Later, we occasionally used the plane to fly up to Seoul for leave or to get supplies. Since pilots were limited in the Pusan Military Government team, I would sometimes fly along as copilot. Maintenance of the plane was inconsistent, and, as a result, it was pretty unreliable. Due to the lack of transportation or even communication—radios provided little more than static—the Pusan Marine Bureau detachment was practically on its own. We had little interference or direction from Seoul.

Inchon, the northern port near Seoul, was the military port where all supplies to support the military would arrive. Pusan was chosen to be the civilian port of entry for Korea. The larger of the two ports, Pusan was more stable and developed. The capital of the South Kyôngsang Province in southeastern South Korea, Pusan is located on the Korea Strait. The second largest South Korean city, with a population of over a million at that time, it was the principal seaport in the country. Later, during the Korean War, Pusan served as the major port of entry and supply depot for the United Nations forces.

For such a large city, Pusan was primitive. The airport was small and barely functional. There were only a few brick buildings. Instead, most were wooden, single-story structures. Only the main roads were paved. In residential areas of the city, as far as you could see were Korean houses, little more than shacks constructed with adjoining walls. Merchants packed their wares in carts, which were pulled around the city by mules. At night, "honey wagons" lit by small oil lamps traveled through the streets collecting human waste to take to the countryside for fertilizer.

The only evidence of the war in Pusan was in the harbor, where extensive bombing from B-29s had destroyed most of the equipment used to load and unload ships. The harbor was also still heavily mined and quite treacherous to those who weren't intimately familiar with it. The port itself was beautiful, a large, natural cove that was protected from storms by breakwaters. Beyond the port, hundreds of tiny islands line Korea's southern coast.

My office was a wooden, two-story building painted white, in total about twice the size of a normal den. Next to it was a one-story communications shack where we kept all of the communications equipment. A third wooden building housed the Port Captain, an Army First Lieutenant, and his assistant, a former Liberty Ship captain, as well as the representative of the Maritime Commission and the Port Doctor. The Port Superintendent, Major Larry Freeborn, and the Port Finance Officer, Lieutenant Wong, were in a large, brick building several blocks away.

Pusan's military government had two teams: one managed the city of Pusan and the other managed the port. I was on the team managing the port. The municipal government provided us with logistics support, particularly in food rations. In turn, we assisted the municipal government when we could by providing firefighting equipment for fires in the city. These trailer pumps were only as effective as the length of their hoses allowed, since they were rigged to pump water directly out of the bay. Unfortunately, many fires in the city were just too far for the equipment to reach.

The Pusan Port Authority team consisted of the Port Superintendent, the Finance Officer, the Port Captain—who was responsible for bringing the ships into the harbor and docking them—an Assistant Port Captain, the Port Doctor, an American civilian who worked for the Federal Maritime Commission and monitored Maritime regulations, and myself.

The Navy ran the Port of Pusan from September 1945

until March 1946, when we took over. The rush to get us all to Pusan was due to the Navy's imminent departure. The Navy Commander in charge was sharp and pragmatic. He had been doing whatever was necessary to keep the port open and its nearly 3,000 Korean laborers, who were unloading the cargo ships, fed. The Koreans, who were filling in for the damaged machinery, would unload grain from the ships, place it in the warehouses, and eventually load it onto railroad cars for transit throughout Korea. As Port Engineer, the Navy Commander explained, I was responsible for getting the food unloaded and onto the trains. Once on the trains, it was entrusted to the Bureau of Railroads.

I was technically supposed to be in charge of the cranes and heavy equipment used to unload ships. But with no parts available to repair the bombed equipment, I was instead responsible for 3,000 manual laborers.

The Navy Commander also calmly informed us that six Japanese ship pilots and their families were under our protection, quite a sticky situation. The Japanese were swiftly deported back to Japan after the war. But we had to secretly hold onto these pilots since they were the only ones who knew where the mines in the port were located. As each ship came in, the Port Captain would take one of these pilots out to safely navigate the mine-filled waters. Also, the port had not been dredged recently, and silt had piled up in many places. Ships could easily run aground if pilots weren't familiar with the deeper route to the wharves.

By keeping the Japanese, we were technically violating the American treaty with the U.S.S.R. to evacuate the Japanese from Korea. The Navy had kept mum about this. Our command in Seoul probably knew about the pilots as well, but also knew we had no alternative. Everyone just stayed quiet about the violation. The Navy had begun the job of training Korean pilots to take over, but in the meantime, they had to keep the Japanese closely guarded in a secret compound. The Navy Commander feared that if the Koreans got access to the Japanese, they would take revenge. The brutal Japanese occupation of Korea had made the Japanese hated enemies.

The responsibility for the pilots' compound fell to me. I kept four men there on a 24-hour guard. We never had an incident, which was lucky, because I wouldn't let our guards have ammunition for their weapons. I felt the risk of a civilian being shot was just too great. As it turned out, the carbines alone were sufficient intimidation. However, if any problems had occurred, we could call upon U.S. Army troops from our occupying infantry division, located nearby, to maintain control and order.

During the two-week transition with the Navy, I learned that our Marine Bureau would also take over a number of vast warehouses that had been stocked by the Navy during its stay. We never had the time or personnel to take inventory, but as Supply Officer, I found sufficient goods there to barter my way into providing what became known as the best mess in South Korea. Everything from Navy-issue P-coats to paint to canned food to spare parts eventually came in handy. When the Navy later came into port, I traded them mostly their own paint for ice cream and occasionally meat and vegetables for my men.

The warehouse also held a treasure of valuable samurai swords. When the Navy first arrived, all the property belonging to the Japanese, especially any weapons, was confiscated. The Japanese were allowed to take with them only what they could carry. One day while the Japanese ship pilots were still at the port, I took one of them, a Japanese Naval Captain, to the warehouse and asked him which sword I should take home with me. I felt honor-bound to take only one. The pilot pointed out a particular short sword. Traditionally, the Japanese carried two swords, one short and one long.

I selected this short one, but later found out that the more valuable swords had wooden covers. Some 20 years later in San Antonio, I sold the sword to a friend who was an antique dealer and bought my son, John, a Remington shotgun with a modified choke to use for skeet shooting. I imagine the Japanese pilot was probably hoping that someday the owners of the swords might come back and get them. Actually, some of the swords did get back to their original owners after restrictions about Japanese possessing weapons became more lenient.

In addition to the Japanese problem, the Navy Commander briefed us on our biggest challenge—feeding the Korean people.

Because the Korean money, the won, was worthless, few Koreans accepted it. The Korean farmers were selling their rice to middlemen for gold, American dollars, or Japanese yen. As a result, there was insufficient rice on the market for the Koreans to survive. Whatever rice was on the local market was expensive, and few could afford it. To avoid a famine, the American government was bringing in American wheat on Liberty Ships. Koreans didn't much care for wheat, but they had little choice. Our daily challenge was to get the wheat unloaded at the port and onto the railroad cars to keep the Koreans fed. The Navy was having a hell of a time unloading these ships because the laborers wanted to be paid in rice, not won, to feed their families. They were given a rice ration, but it wasn't enough to feed their families.

"You must get more rice for the laborers," the Navy Commander emphatically told us, "and you can't get it from the federal government in Seoul because they have limited supplies. You must get it yourselves."

He then proceeded to tell us an incredible story about how he and his men had managed to keep the port open. Smugglers were transporting the rice on sampans to Japan. The U.S. Navy was on patrol, but with the low profile of the wooden sampans, the Navy ships' radar was almost useless. Most of the smugglers were successful. They just hid in coves until dark and then crossed the Tsushima Strait to Japan.

"We have an LCVP [a small landing craft] with a large floodlight that we are going to leave with you," the Commander explained. "We take it out at night and look for the smugglers in the coves along the shore. When we find them, we confiscate the rice, kick the crews off, and either sink the sampans, damage them, or leave them on one of the islands. We bring back the rice and put it in the warehouse to pay our laborers. It is the only way we have found to provide the extra rice in the quantities necessary."

All of us listening to the story were shocked at the illicit operation described by the Navy Commander. They were raiding the smugglers! And little did we realize that we were soon going to be doing the very same thing.

"Forget it," the Port Superintendent told the Navy Commander. "That is a court-martial offense. That's not my responsibility. I am not going to do it." That said, he left. He didn't want to hear any more or be involved. But I instinctively knew that he had not said for me to do the same. If I had been caught, he could say truthfully that he did not know of the operations. He never placed any obstacles in my path.

After the Port Superintendent left, the Navy Commander told me very seriously that if we didn't take over the rice raids, we would soon be without any laborers. "Without them, Korea is going to find itself in a famine," he said. "Many thousands will die." Then he took it one step further. "If a famine does occur, we might lose South Korea to the North Koreans and the Soviets."

North Korean communist infiltrators and guerrillas were just beginning to cause problems in the South, attempting to get the South Koreans to lose faith in the American government and support the North. Though I was more influenced by the idea of saving lives from famine than by the possible political threat, I understood that choosing to become a midnight raider or not was a decision with serious repercussions.

All Work and Some Play, Korea, 1946-1947

CHAPTER FOUR

The last thing the Navy did before heading out was turn over their houses to us. The port was surrounded by homes built by Japanese millionaires. Overlooking the harbor, most of them were two-story structures in traditional Japanese style with straw mats on the floors and beautifully painted sliding doors separating the rooms. I shared a house with the U.S. Maritime representative and our Finance Officer. Between us we had six Korean houseboys.

As second in command, I had the pick of any house near the port; the Port Superintendent had chosen to live in a mansion at the top of a hill in town. The house I chose was great, but I immediately thought I had too many houseboys. Six just seemed like so many. The Navy Lieutenant who was moving out told me I had to keep them. "If you let any of them go, they will starve to death," he said. So they stayed to guard and clean the house and do our laundry.

I never really went into the back of the house where they lived and worked until shortly before I left Korea. When I did venture there, I found several women and many small chil-

My first house in Pusan, compliments of the Japanese.

dren. I asked the houseboys for an explanation, and learned that the house "boys" were older than I thought they were. These were their wives and children. They had been afraid to tell me about them in fear that I would kick them out, which would have meant certain starvation for their families.

I only wished I had learned about them earlier, because I could have gotten them milk, bread, and more food for their families. I never would have made them leave. I only used the front rooms and my bedroom on the second floor. Even with two roommates, there was plenty of space to go around.

Our accommodations were really wonderful with the exception of the bathroom facilities. One of the first remodeling jobs we accomplished on the house was to install an American-type box toilet with a toilet seat. Later, in a second house, we rigged an old airplane fuel tank up on a platform to make a shower. Koreans, like the Japanese, had only large, coal-heated tubs for bathing with the whole family. We added a hand-pump for our well so that the houseboys could pump the water up to the tank on the tower. Gravity created a shower. We had limited hot water, but the shower was entirely adequate. Ours being the only house in town with an enclosed shower, we became quite popular with some of the American nurses at the military hospital in Pusan who missed the comforts of home.

We moved to this second home, interestingly, when the Major General in command of the division, stationed not far from Pusan, decided he wanted to live off of the base. He sent his Adjutant to Pusan to search for quarters with instructions to find a home with a view of the port. Our first house was the best to be had, so we were out.

Music made both of our houses favorite destinations. When I came to Korea, I brought over a record player. Packed with two straps and a handle, I had to carry it all the way from Virginia. It was a burden on the way, but it paid off. It may have been one of the only record players in all of Korea at the time. The music made socializing with the nurses a lot more fun. We put on big-band records, and the living room became our dance floor. When no one was around, I spent time listening to my favorite music—big bands and the fast-paced Spanish bullfighting marches called *paso dobles*.

Settled into my second home, I began to learn more about my job. Jack-of-all-trades might have been the best title to describe the myriad responsibilities—Engineering Officer, Supply Officer, Communications Officer, Housing Officer, and Executive Officer all rolled into one. I was the last of the six-officer team to arrive, and, as the Executive Officer, I had to find the skilled enlisted men necessary to operate the port.

The Major in charge of the port was kept busy back at Port Headquarters in Pusan. Every morning, a line of Koreans stretched around the block trying to get in to see him. One after the other, they tried to convince him to give them parts of the port infrastructure left behind by the Japanese—fishing ships, boats, houses, and other property. At the time of surrender and evacuation, the Japanese lost all property rights. What was left behind had to be sorted out by the victorious Allies—the spoils of war. It was up to the Major to distribute the equipment, including many fine small yachts in the port. This alone was a full-time job. Some of the Koreans had documentation of previous Japanese confiscation or some verification of an interest in property that went generations back. Others signed notes to buy or rent various properties. These yachts stayed in the harbor fully staffed, and we couldn't get rid of the crews because they would starve to death. We had to feed them, too. The Port Captain and I occasionally took American soldiers from the hospital out on short cruises on these yachts. It was good R&R, Rest & Recuperation, for all of us. During one of these cruises, I met a young nurse named Betty, who I liked from the start.

To recruit the men we needed to run the port, I had to go to the 5th Infantry Division outside of Pusan. The port officers had decided on the kinds and numbers of personnel required. With this list in hand, I went to the Division Commander and told him I had the authority of General Lerch and General Hodge to find the men I needed. General Lerch was the commander of the military government. General Hodge was commander of the XXIV Corps and the overall commander. Though the Division Commander was reluctant to let go of skilled men, he had no choice due to the orders from above. So I went from company to company and addressed the troops with my list of jobs, not forgetting to add that we had good food.

The number of skills you could find in any ordinary infantry division in the American Army was amazing. Those who were interested gave their names to the company clerk. Within a week, they were transferred to the Port Authority. Since this was postwar, many veterans had returned home. The men who stayed were mostly privates, but they didn't lack skills.

I found several wireless operators, mechanics, stevedore supervisors, military police, warehousemen, cooks, and one outstanding diesel mechanic who kept us alive when we began our rice raids by keeping our small, unreliable boat at least semiseaworthy. The Landing Craft Vehicle Personnel, or LCVP, was the smallest of the Navy landing craft designed to carry two jeeps and a platoon of men. It had practically no draft and sat almost on top of the water, so we didn't worry about it being beached. The front of the ship opened up so troops could easily reach the beach. On our midnight missions, we never needed to take advantage of this feature. What the LCVP didn't have was a decent engine, but our mechanic on board vastly improved our odds.

What I couldn't find in the infantry division located outside of Pusan was enough wireless operators who knew Morse code. I eventually hired two Koreans who had worked for the Japanese. They didn't have a place to live, so I also had to find them quarters. These men became invaluable. Professionals, they not only knew Morse code, but were also trilingual, speaking Korean, Japanese, and passable English. The United States had given many of the Liberty Ships that docked at Pusan to Korea. Since they were staffed with Korean crews, knowledge of Korean was essential.

The communications experts kept the port operating. Ships far away had to be reached by Morse code via wireless communications. Closer, in line of sight, we could use very high-frequency radios for voice communications. In addition to civilian traffic, we had to communicate with the Navy since it used Pusan as a base for patrols, as well as to refurbish ships.

After the personnel had been recruited, and in the ensuing week while the paperwork was being processed to transfer the men, I had to find permanent quarters for the company of 200 men. We examined numerous unused Japanese facilities before deciding on one on the outskirts of Pusan—a former school for Japanese girls. It was designed in a square, like a fort, with a white brick wall along all four sides. The walls were not tall enough to prevent a determined man with a ladder from climbing over them. It had a single, gated entrance. The dormitories were in the center. The warehouses for supplies and food lockers for perishables were along one side. It had a small pool instead of a tower where water was stored for reserve. The girl's school made more than sufficient quarters.

Two Korean guards stood at the entrance at all times. Any

time I entered the compound, the guards bowed low and humbly. The practice was always embarrassing to me, and I never got used to it. No matter how much I tried to dissuade them, it was an ingrained habit. The Koreans were used to the Japanese. If they had not bowed to a Japanese officer, they could expect a blow from the side of a sword as a reminder. Another practice I tried to avoid was the custom in many commands to post the portrait of the existing commander in a prominent location. When I was the senior officer, I insisted on using the portrait of my immediate superior instead.

The two sergeants in charge of the compound asked my permission to hire some houseboys. Finding room for the boys in the compound was no problem, finding extra food was.

The municipal government was responsible for providing rations to the men of the Port Authority. The rations barely covered the Americans, much less the Korean staff. What we got was poor quality, mostly canned food with some vegetables and fruit. As Supply Officer, I constantly worried whether or not sufficient food would be available, and I had to be ever on the lookout for supplements.

When an American cargo ship arrived, the Port Captain and I went aboard to welcome the officers and take care of any formalities. The Port Captain was on official business. I tried to appear to be on official business, but in reality I was on board for one and only one purpose—getting extra food. While the Port Captain talked with the ship's Captain, I pulled aside one of the senior officers and asked him what they needed.

I first offered my home—there were few other places they could go to get a break from being on the ship for weeks. Then I moved on to my jeep.

Invariably, one of my suggestions sounded great to them, and at that moment, I let them know about our shortages.

"Of course, we have a little problem here. We don't get any fresh food. We hardly get any vegetables or fruit or meat. Can you help us out?"

Typically, the officers were hesitant. These were merchant fleets with union officials on board who were very strict about this sort of thing. But I usually wore them down.

"I'll tell you what," they'd finally say. "Let's get together later tonight. You bring your LCVP over on the right side away from the wharf, and I'll see what I can do."

Any such trading had to be done at night from the ocean side not the wharf side. If a union official had seen an officer taking crates of meat, fruits, and vegetables, there could have been dire consequences. Thus, the trading was always done very quietly and secretively, in the dead of night.

If the ships needed certain naval supplies, I checked the warehouse and negotiated with those. Sometimes I traded samurai swords for food. It was not unusual to have two or three officers staying temporarily at our home. But it was all easy payment for several cases of meat or fresh vegetables that lasted us days. With three or four ships in our harbor at any one time, we generally ate well, and our Korean helpers did also. When I couldn't get extra food—and there were times when none was to be had—we were left to rations that had to be spread thin to cover us and the Koreans in our compound.

When the word got out about the quality of our mess, the local Railroad Bureau Commander came to me with his officers to negotiate a deal. After that, we received their rations and, in return, they ate at our mess. The railroad detachment got the better end of that bargain. However, afterward I did receive the utmost cooperation from them.

The Navy also helped to supplement our table. Naval personnel had plenty of whiskey; they just couldn't open it on board ship. Often the officers came up to our house and had a great time drinking and singing and partying, occasionally with the nurses. In return we got ice cream and sometimes meat. It was a very heady time for me, a young First Lieutenant, to be entertaining senior naval officers who commanded destroyers and cruisers. Sitting there in full braid, they were quite an eyeful for a young, impressionistic officer.

We got particularly lucky when the Commander-in-Chief of the Pacific fleet ordered the ships painted a certain color of gray. We just happened to have a warehouse full of this variety of gray paint. That order kept us in ice cream for the duration. Imagine trading $10,000 worth of paint for a few gallons of ice cream. Of course, the paint belonged to the Navy in the first place.

The Navy also provided us with a significant advantage in Pusan's romance derby by leaving us their jeeps. Obviously, it was far more romantic to go out on a date in a jeep than in a two-and-a-half-ton truck. In addition to the military nurses, from time to time the USO would come to Pusan. One of the prettiest USO girls was a trumpet player I had the opportunity to date. She was great looking and may not have given me the time of day except for my situation—I had a large house with a staff and, most importantly, that jeep. Before she left, I took her to the warehouse at the port and loaded her up with souvenirs—vases, jade, and a sword left behind by the Japanese. There were literally millions of dollars of collectibles in that warehouse and absolutely no accountability as to where it all went.

Pusan was not exactly paradise for the 12 nurses and three Red Cross girls stationed at the military hospital, but we did our best to entertain them. Inevitably, several of us ended up competing for one girl. This was the case with Betty, the nurse I met on an outing with the soldiers from the hospital. When I met her, Betty was dating a hospital dentist. Luckily, tours at that time were relatively short, and the dentist left for stateside within a few months. Between boyfriends, both the Port Superintendent and I quickly pursued her. She and I were closer together in age; the Port Superintendent was about 10 years our senior. Eventually, I won out, and we went steady for the rest of my tour in Korea.

I thought of marrying her, but I was still insecure. I'd seen too many junior officers marry who were not financially secure and whose duties made them less-than-perfect husbands.

After all, I was still a reserve officer. At the time, 90 percent of the officers were reserve officers. Regular officers generally were West Pointers. As a reserve officer, my military career was somewhat insecure. Also, it was a great time to be single and footloose. I was in no hurry to marry. Eventually, she got tired of waiting for me. We saw each other infrequently when we both got home.

My success with women was initially somewhat of a surprise to me. When I was a child, a little girl I had admired from afar criticized me for having a dirty shirt. This was a strong blow to my fragile ego, and I carried it with me. Several years later, another little girl I had a crush on stopped me on the street. She was wheeling a baby carriage and pointed to the doll inside. "This is our baby," she told me. I was flabbergasted. I had never imagined that she returned my affection. Later in life, when I felt insecure about women, I tried to remember that you never really know what they are thinking.

Life in Pusan was not one continuous date. We had to work hard—often seven days a week, 10 and 12 hours a day. Sometimes I couldn't tell what hour or day of the week it was. They all began to blend together. Ships came in that had to be unloaded regardless of whether it was Monday morning or Friday night. But we felt good about the work. Millions of Koreans were being fed because of the efforts of just a few Americans. The Koreans were grateful and welcomed all that we did to help. Very few of us ever carried guns, which is an indication of the popularity Americans enjoyed among the Korean people.

I worked with many fine Koreans during my time in Pusan. One especially trusted Korean was in charge of all of the unloading laborers at the port. I made sure he had enough rice for payday and told him to go find the laborers. Although he was certainly left with considerable room to carve out personal gain, he got the job done, so I didn't ask questions. I also had a Korean interpreter, Kim, who went everywhere I went. He was a hard worker and extremely reliable. I trusted him implicitly.

Eventually, the rice stores left by the Navy began to dwindle, and the time came when we had to begin the rice raids. This duty quickly became a favorite among the enlisted men, and we eventually used it as a reward for hard work. When we went out, I selected several soldiers to accompany me. My interpreter and our diesel genius were always on board. Without this mechanic, it's doubtful these exploits ever would have succeeded.

We knew on moonless nights that the sampans hid in any one of a thousand coves along the Korean shoreline, waiting to take their goods to Japan. MacArthur knew about the smugglers and had ordered a flotilla of destroyers to patrol the strait. But the sampans were wooden and didn't reflect radar beams, making them virtually invisible to the destroyers. Thus, the majority of the smugglers succeeded, despite the patrols. But we got our share.

I was never worried about any type of threat from the smugglers themselves. The real threat was the unreliability of the LCVP. If the small craft had broken down and we had been discovered, it would have ended our military careers. Storms were also a major threat. In a best-case scenario, we would have to beach the LCVP and walk miles back to the port.

In the beginning, we went out on weekly raids. The crew would leave just after midnight. I gave all of the soldiers carbines but no ammunition. I always carried a .45 pistol with five rounds, but I never had to fire it. We silently patrolled the many small coves along the southern shore of South Korea. When we heard something or saw something, we hit the floodlight. Typically, the smugglers dropped flat onto the deck of the sampan. Used to the harsh Japanese control and expecting to be beaten or killed, the Koreans repeatedly bowed and begged for mercy. Kim would quickly make it very clear that we were not interested in killing or hurting them. We just wanted the rice.

All Work and Some Play, Korea, 1946-1947

While the Navy had made it a practice to sometimes sink the sampans when the crews were slow to cooperate, I decided early on to let them go, sort of my own catch and release policy. If they got away, we could raid them another day. After all, I knew we could never stop all the smuggling.

A good haul was more than 50 100-pound bags of rice per sampan. Some nights we came back empty-handed, other nights we caught as many as three or four smugglers. The men would point their unloaded carbines, and the most I ever had to do was make the smugglers aware of my side arm. If any of the smugglers had ever resisted—which they didn't—we would not have pursued them. If we shot any Koreans or if any of my men had been hurt as a consequence of the raids, there's no doubt I would have been court-martialed. Luckily, our bluff always worked. And the smugglers could not turn us in because they, themselves, were operating illegally.

I instructed my men to be firm but not abusive with the smugglers, and usually they complied. But one night, my best company cook pushed one of the Koreans into the water and thrust his carbine into another smuggler's chest. When I rebuffed him, he turned to me and said, "They're only gooks."

"It's their country. We're the visitors here," I told him. "We're not here to hurt anybody, and if you do that one more time I'll transfer you."

Since our conditions were so much better than anywhere else, and the rice raids were coveted perks, this was no idle threat. Later I noticed the cook's unacceptable habit of driving down the local roads and knocking off the oversized *papasan* hats of Koreans walking alongside. I made good on my threat then and transferred him.

Eventually, the situation in Korea improved. The government became more stable and the currency began to hold some value. With confidence in the won, our workers began to accept it instead of rice. Better control of the rice harvest led to surpluses, and finally, the raids were no longer needed. Though the raids certainly had been exciting, the LCVP was on its last leg. I finally decided our luck had held long enough and stopped the midnight adventures. We still had plenty of challenges ahead.

The American government had given Liberty Ships to the Korean government, which manned them with Korean sailors. Most of the Koreans had gained their experience on Japanese vessels where they weren't permitted to organize unions. The senior Maritime Commission member in Seoul, accustomed to unions, talked the Military Governor into allowing one. He believed a Korean union was essential for the merchant marine fleet to operate democratically and efficiently. As you might expect, the new union leaders visited all of the ships given to them by Americans and created immediate discontent with the rice rations and wages being paid. They then went to Seoul to ask for better conditions from the American military government.

Too late, the Americans realized they had a problem. When the American military government refused the union demands, the Koreans called a strike. The Korean seamen, following instructions, pulled into the nearest harbor, docked, and stayed on their ships, refusing to leave.

Pusan was the primary port of destination for most Korean vessels, being the civilian support port. Inchon was for military occupation support. It was not unusual to have four or five of these ships in Pusan at one time. When the strike first broke out, the Chief of the Marine Bureau called our Port Superintendent and told him to organize a meeting of the strikers in Pusan to try to talk them into agreeing with the American conditions. The Port Superintendent called the ships' officers and union representatives to his office for a meeting.

He was unyielding. "We are not going to recognize the strike," he told them.

I had been a part of the meeting and quickly saw that the American position was unfair. The Korean requests were basic—they wanted some security, better food, and better living conditions. Nothing unreasonable.

I was sympathetic to their cause and, out of earshot of the Koreans, said to the Superintendent, "You know, why don't we give them a little bit?"

"Listen, Bill," he replied, "I don't have any choice. I've been told not to give. Also, they've told me to deactivate the communications on each ship so they can't communicate with each other."

Seoul had instructed the Pusan port authorities to tie up the ships in the harbor to prevent them from leaving and to disable their communications. As Communications Officer, I got that dirty job. The Assistant Port Captain was a former captain of a Liberty Ship, so I went to him for advice.

"I don't know where their radio shacks are," I told him.

"I'll take you up there," he offered.

We went on board each of the ships to fulfill Seoul's orders. Far from an expert on ship communications, I knew enough about radios to know which tubes were the essential components. I didn't want to permanently disable the communications even though those were my orders. I knew the strike had to be over in a week or two. For me to destroy all this valuable equipment didn't make sense. But I felt I had to obey the spirit of the orders, even if I didn't go by the book. After all, I have not always been a by the book kind of guy.

I severed communications by taking a power vacuum tube out of each of the radios on board each of the ships. However, instead of destroying them, I just put each tube in a nearby drawer, locked each office, and gave the keys to the Assistant Port Captain.

"Did you deactivate them?" he asked.

"Yep. I deactivated them," was the extent of my reply. Experienced operators could have replaced the tubes easily and had the radios working again within the hour. But the Port Superintendent was happy, the Seoul government was satisfied, and I had avoided what I felt was a potentially disastrous situation. Shortly afterward, the parties reached a compromise and the seamen went back to work.

A week after the strike was over, the senior union representative in Pusan and several other union officials came to my office. Closing the door, they bowed as was their custom and thanked me for being sympathetic to their cause. They presented me with a beautifully engraved antique sterling-silver replica of a "honey wagon" like those used to transport waste from the city to the farms. I still treasure the gift to this day. When I returned stateside, I gave the silver honey wagon to my sister's adopted parents because they collected sterling silver. When they died, it was returned to me.

Though some GIs treated the Koreans like they were "just gooks," I sincerely liked the Korean people. Once when I was driving my jeep, I got stuck in the mud in the middle of nowhere. I sat there for a few minutes wondering just how I was going to get out of this one without a long walk. Soon a squad of Korean soldiers on a truck came along. They saw me in my immobile jeep, and, without even being asked, got out of their truck, pulled me out of the mud, and put me back on the road. I was grateful. When I thanked them, they just replied in pidgin English, "We are all brothers together." Their simple words made a lasting impression on me.

During the rest of my stay in Pusan, I continued to try to deal with the Korean people, keeping those words in mind. One night, several Korean kids, three boys and a girl, attempted to break into the food locker on our compound. Guards intercepted them and beat them. When the incident was reported to me while in progress, I told my men to stop the beating and to let the kids go. The Koreans were having a hard time finding food, and, despite everything we were trying to do to get the country working again, they often went hungry.

A Sergeant from the Office of Special Investigations later questioned me about the incident.

"We heard you had a robbery here," he said to me.

"Yes, but we took care of it," I told him.

"You're suppose to report these things to us, Lieutenant," I was told. I had not reported the incident because I felt being beaten had been sufficient punishment. The Sergeant wanted more information on the would-be robbers and wanted me to arrest the offenders for them.

"Look, we got rid of them. They're gone. We don't know who they were. We don't have any way of getting them back. Let's just forget it ever happened," was my response.

Perhaps I was sympathetic to the Koreans because they made me remember an incident in my own life when I was still working with the CCC. One of my best friends was assigned to the officers' kitchen and had a key to the food cellar. Young boys, we were always hungry. One night about 2 a.m., we opened up the food cellar and cooked more eggs than you can possibly imagine. I was always surprised I didn't get sick.

The OSI detectives in Korea were not too pleased with my attitude, but they never did anything more about it. Eventually the incident faded away. The OSI had considerable authority and could have made life difficult for us. We were still conducting the rice raids at the time, and if these men had investigated and discovered our illicit operations, we would have been in serious trouble. I treated them nicely but cautiously. Their job was to secure the area and to follow the letter of the law. But my counterparts and I recognized that there were many special circumstances in a postwar situation. The letter of the law didn't take into account the realities of the day.

I rarely had to make any show of force with the Korean people, and only did so when I thought it was absolutely necessary. In one case, my interpreter was found by Korean police after curfew and placed in a Korean jail. When I found out, I went to the jail along with another Korean. He told the policeman who I was and the name of my interpreter who was in custody.

"Yes, we have him," the Desk Sergeant said.

"I'd like to have him out," I replied. "He works for me and must be on the job tomorrow. He holds an important position that is critical to the port."

Like many bureaucrats, the Desk Sergeant was afraid to do anything outside of his defined authority. He shook his head no. "I can't release him until the judge releases him," he said.

The Sergeant and the Korean I'd brought along began arguing. I had heard from other Koreans that the police had beat up my interpreter, so I asked the Korean to ask the policeman if Kim was all right.

"Well, he resisted arrest. We had to beat him a little bit," we were told.

"What kind of shape is he in?" I asked.

"Well, pretty good. We're not too worried about him."

"Yes, I know. But I'd like to see him anyway."

"Well, you know, you can't see him unless I get the authority from my senior officer who's not here."

"I'd like to see him," I said one last time, opening the flap to my .45. "Tell him I'm going to see him," I instructed the Korean interpreter who was with me.

The policeman, seeing an American officer as mad as I was, decided to take me to see Kim. Of course I was acting a bluff, and I hoped it would work. I found Kim in a small, dirty cell with straw on the floor and a swollen face.

"Get up and come with me," I told him. I was really worried about his condition and his safety, as well as his future.

"No, no, no. I can't do that. They'll shoot me for attempting to escape," Kim pleaded.

"Don't worry. You just stay in front of me. I will be behind you. Let's get out of here."

I put my arms around him, and we slowly started for the front door. The Desk Sergeant didn't know what to do. On the one hand he had his responsibility to his superiors and the law. On the other hand, he had an armed American officer demanding the release of his prisoner. We walked out with no further problems. Later, I was thankful it was a Korean policeman on duty. If it had been an American at the desk, I don't think we would have gotten away with my tough act.

All Work and Some Play, Korea, 1946-1947

In another episode, when I moved into my second house, I found that a Korean family was illegally living there. I felt like it was my obligation to find them another place to live, so I told my interpreter to make sure they had a place to go before we moved them.

One night at about 2 a.m., the father of the family came to me in a panic. The man didn't speak English, but through motions and a few Korean words, I understood that a poisonous snake had apparently bitten his wife, who had come along with him. I immediately put the couple into my jeep and took them over to the American military hospital.

"We just can't take her," the American doctor on duty told me. "We have a small hospital here with only five doctors. The precedence would be horrible. There are a million Koreans in Pusan. If we start taking Korean patients, we will be flooded with Koreans, and we won't be able to take care of the Americans. You better take her to the civilian hospital up the road."

That was our next stop, but we couldn't find any doctors in the hospital after searching the emergency room and many corridors. Finally, I saw a man in a white jacket who was walking down a hallway. He was about 50 years old and turned out to be a doctor.

I brought the couple over and pointed to the bite on the wife's arm. The doctor was nonplused. He didn't say a thing and started to walk away.

"Bring him back here," I told the husband. "I want him to take care of her."

The doctor again shrugged his shoulders and continued to walk away.

I immediately unbuckled the flap on my holster and said again emphatically, "Take care of her."

I turned to her husband, who could speak some English, and instructed him to tell the doctor what I was saying. The doctor froze when he saw the open flap to my .45. He instantly became cooperative. He looked at her arm, put some antiseptic salve on the wound, and gave her a shot. I wouldn't have used the pistol, but the doctor didn't know that. Several days later, I asked Kim to go to the couple's house and find out how the woman was doing. He returned to tell me that she was fine.

Pusan was a learning experience for me. It's sometimes hard to believe I had so much authority at such a young age. Often I had to abandon "the book" and rely upon my own judgment. Two such experiences involved our responsibility of food distribution. Once we received a big shipment of Almond Roca candy instead of the usual sugar shipment that we were supposed to hand over to the railroad people to be given to the Koreans. Though I certainly wouldn't keep anything from them that they needed, I felt like distributing expensive candy to the Korean people was overdoing it. I held back the candy, though I didn't necessarily have the authority to do it. We used some of it to trade for other food for our mess and sent the rest to the military hospital.

Another time we received a shipment of wheat that was packed in Soviet grain sacks. Though the Soviets had been our allies in World War II, the antagonistic relationship between Soviet-occupied North Korea and U.S.-occupied South Korea was escalating. There was no way I was going to let these South Koreans think the Soviets were feeding them. We scrounged the city until we found enough Korean rice bags to use for the wheat, and then we repacked every last one of them.

During the time I served in the military government, I commanded many men deserving of promotion, but one of the few soldiers I did promote was my driver. I later regretted this. The Corporal was a good soldier, effective and reliable, but not any more so than a number of others. The simple fact that he was close to me resulted in his promotion. Many other men, such as my wireless operators, were much more valuable than this driver was, but they didn't have the opportunity to develop a relationship with me. My driver earned his stripes simply because I liked him. In the military, as elsewhere, life is not always fair.

Our superior in the Marine Bureau in Seoul never did visit Pusan. Only once did any senior official visit us. He was the Senior Civil Servant, the number two man in the Department of Transportation from Seoul, and the son of a U.S. Ambassador. Since the Port Superintendent was busy and couldn't provide this man with the VIP treatment expected, he asked me to take care of him. I invited him to stay at my house, let him use my jeep, and introduced him to some nurses from the hospital.

The official was very flattered by the attention and told me he thought I was doing a great job in Pusan.

"I'll tell the Colonel when I get up to Seoul, and I'm going to recommend you for the Army Commendation Medal," he told me.

I told him it really wasn't necessary.

"No matter," the official said, "I'll see to it." He returned to Seoul and gave me a highly favorable review.

At the end of my tour, just as I was ready to leave for Kimpo Air Force Base near Seoul to fly stateside, the official called me and asked me to stop in to see him in Seoul on my way home.

I expected I was headed to Seoul to receive my Army Commendation Medal, but at the time, I was more interested in planning a special rendezvous with my girlfriend, who was already in Seoul at a conference. I didn't have any way of getting around in Seoul to meet with this girl, and was determined to get us some transportation.

A new Port Superintendent had just arrived in Pusan and was still pretty dependent on me. I told him we ought to take a jeep up to Inchon to get parts for our LCVP and other supplies for the port before I left.

"While I'm in Inchon, I'll get those parts and have the driver bring them back," I offered. "I'll get the requisitions while I'm in Seoul."

The Port Superintendent agreed, not knowing my motivation was to have transportation available in Seoul for romancing my girlfriend and in Inchon to get the parts.

The only way to get the jeep to Seoul was to tie it onto a flatbed trailer on a railroad car. Since Seoul hadn't authorized the trip, I couldn't get my driver a ticket to sit in the passenger car of the train with me. The only way I could get the jeep back to Pusan with the supplies, since I was headed back to the States, was to have the driver go up there with me. I asked him if he wanted to go to Seoul for a while, and of course he did. He wanted to see the town, and when I didn't have a date, he would have access to the jeep.

Unfortunately, he was going to be on that freight car for about 12 hours. The train from Pusan to Seoul stopped frequently. The locomotives were still not in the best of shape, and the tracks weren't always solid, so the train had to travel slowly. The jeep and its driver were placed on the train in a freight car. When we finally arrived in Seoul, the driver was exhausted, hungry, and covered with soot.

I used that jeep often the first few days and was quite conspicuous since almost all the officers in Seoul drove two-and-a-half-ton trucks, not jeeps. I couldn't help but be noticed, and it wasn't long before word got back to the Chief of the Marine Bureau, Lieutenant Colonel Nelson.

"Hey, Cracken's really living it up with that jeep of his," an officer told him.

The Lieutenant Colonel, who was my immediate superior, called me in. What ensued was really embarrassing.

"Bill, what the hell are you doing with a jeep up here?" he asked me.

"I brought it up here to get supplies in Inchon," was my excuse. "You can check with the Port Superintendent."

The Lieutenant Colonel was dubious, so later I called the Port Superintendent in Pusan and asked him to be sure to call the Lieutenant Colonel and tell him why I was there. But it was too late. My story was transparent to the more-experienced Lieutenant Colonel.

"Don't you realize that we are running a business here?"

he asked me. "When you put that jeep on that train, somebody has to be charged for freight. This is not a freebie even if you put supplies on that jeep of yours. You'll owe us for that ride. I ought to court-martial you."

The Army never billed me, and obviously, I wasn't court-martialed, though I certainly could have been. The Lieutenant Colonel sent the driver back to Pusan with the supplies, but kept the jeep for himself. It was a learning experience I have always remembered. In the eyes of the Army, one stupid move wiped out all of the good work I had accomplished in Pusan. At the time, though, I was not overly concerned. With our own jeep, my girlfriend and I had a great time during those last few days in Seoul.

I never heard another word about my Army Commendation Medal, and I was only slightly disappointed. After all, I was leaving Korea for the United States to get out of the service. I thought I was through with the Army and Korea for good.

Searching for Home,
Stateside, 1947-1950

CHAPTER FIVE

College was on my mind as I walked into the Administration Office at Travis Air Force Base to begin the process of becoming a civilian. When I was asked my home of record, I naturally said "New York." Though I didn't have stirring emotional ties to the city, it was the only home I had ever known.

"We have a troop train heading east to New York and Pennsylvania, full of soldiers returning from the Pacific," the Major in charge told me. "Lieutenant Cracken, you're assigned as the mess officer aboard this troop train."

With few officers available, it was a fair assignment, but I didn't want to end my military career as a mess officer. To say the least, this was bad news. If I could help it, I wasn't going to have the job of making sure everyone got fed on a troop train traveling across the country. So I went back to Administration and changed my home of record to California. Now I could receive my discharge papers there. Still, I really wanted to get to the East Coast to see my sister and my Aunt Em and Uncle John.

Pondering the future, I headed to the Officers' Club at

Travis Air Force Base the night before my discharge papers became effective. There I had the good fortune to chat with a Warrant Officer about my situation.

"This is your lucky day," he told me. "I am the only one in this whole area who can help you."

It was my lucky day. He was the Assistant Adjutant General at the base in charge of transportation for discharged veterans. He changed my orders and gave me a voucher to fly home. Instead of traveling among potato peelings in the mess car of a slow-moving train, I flew first class on a commercial airplane to New York.

Growing up, Aunt Em and Uncle John Viscardi loved me the only way they knew how. Both dedicated professionals, he an engineer and she a doctor, raising a little boy was not part of their plan. But when my mother died of cancer, there I was, along with my older sister, Sara, on their doorstep. They soon found a home for Sara where she could be a governess of sorts. She grew to love her adopted family and they her, while I grew up in a cold, businesslike environment with my aunt and uncle. I vividly remember Aunt Em's greeting upon my return from the South Pacific: "I am glad you're back, but I don't believe in wars," she said curtly.

"Aunt Em, if I hadn't gone to war and the rest of us hadn't gone to war, you'd probably be a lot worse off than you are now," was my reply.

I was not too surprised by this greeting, but I knew I would not feel comfortable living with them. I did stay for a few days, though, and bought them their first television set. I bought a second set for Margaret, their black housekeeper, who had really brought me up. As a boy, I spent many cozy evenings eating dinner in the kitchen with Margaret while my aunt and uncle dined out. When Aunt Em and I walked out of that television store, she said, "That salesman really talked you into that television set."

"Aunt Em," I said, "we were going in there to buy you one. He didn't talk us into anything."

That was just Aunt Em.

After those few days in New York, I began to realize that I missed the military. It had become my home. I was restless, and the spirit of adventure was still driving me to search for something beyond the mundane. Although the GI Bill provided the means for me to go to college, it didn't pay enough to live comfortably—only $50 a month. At the time, I estimated that my savings would provide me extra funds for only about six months. Though I really wanted to finish my degree in engineering, Aunt Em and Uncle John never volunteered to subsidize me. They wanted me to be independent. And somehow, being a student seemed too passive after my experiences in the South Pacific and Korea.

I had a friend working at Wright-Patterson Air Force Base in Dayton, Ohio. He worked for an Army Air Forces contractor and had a reasonable salary, and he encouraged me to head his way. I figured I could build up my savings while I was there and then go back to college later. Since I already had some engineering background and Wright-Patterson was the engineering center for the Army Air Forces, I was hired by the civilian contractor as a research officer.

In early 1947, the Army Air Forces was busy evaluating all the documents salvaged from Germany at the end of World War II. As the troops advanced into Germany, we gathered anything that could be of value to the military—documents, armaments, and even scientists. When I got to Wright-Patterson, there were buildings literally full of blueprints and documents. No one knew what we had. My job was to sit at a desk on the dusty, windowless third floor of a building, poring over old German blueprints. I was one member of a team assembled to evaluate the usefulness of what had been brought back from the war. Sometimes we would find specifications from the German jets and missiles program. My team specifically was looking for new features on missiles or avionics that we didn't recognize. If we found something interesting, we'd send the documents on to another team of specialists for a more detailed analysis. It was a very slow process, and the surroundings were dismal. More often than not, the documents I reviewed were worthless.

Tired and bored after about six months of being elbow-deep in dirty blueprints, I went to the Military Personnel Department in Washington and requested permission to be recalled to active duty as a Reserve Officer, this time in the U.S. Air Force. I had applied at just the right time. By 1948, so many people had left the armed forces that the Air Force, which was now a separate armed force from the Army, needed experienced officers. I had heard that you could be in the military and go to school at the same time, and that was my plan.

I was first sent to Lowry Air Force Base in Denver for a refresher course in aircraft maintenance. Upon completion of that course, I was assigned to Williams Air Force Base outside of Chandler, Arizona, to the Fighter Gunnery School. At Williams, fighter pilots were trained in advanced fighter tactics and gunnery techniques, many of which had been developed as a result of experience gained during World War II. Day and night, pilots were practicing firing machine guns and missiles and bombing in order to build their air-to-surface interdiction skills on a firing range in the desert.

The school was fascinating and gratifying. I was the Assistant Aircraft Maintenance Officer for the school and was responsible for keeping the aircraft flying and the avionics and guns in working condition. Our primary aircraft was the P-51 Mustang, however, we also flew and maintained the F-80, one of the earliest jets. I met many fine pilots there, including Bob Knapp, a fighter ace during World War II who I would later meet again in Norway. I settled in to Williams, coaching the swim team and getting to know the area. I have always loved to swim and had been an active competitor as a boy.

During my tour at Williams, the Commanding General was moved to Goodfellow Air Force Base in San Angelo, Texas, to become its commander. Goodfellow was a flight-training base that was closed after World War II, and in 1948, the Air Force decided to reactivate the base to train pilots. The General had to start from scratch, so he recruited officers from Williams. When he made his list, I was on it. I wanted to stay at Williams, but didn't get the choice. In retrospect, I'm glad I wasn't left behind. At Goodfellow, I met Lieutenant Bob Gross, who became one of my best friends. I also learned to trust my instincts through a lesson I would never forget.

One day, my Squadron Commander, who I liked very much, came in fighting mad.

"I came through the front gate and had to wait 30 minutes before I got in," he said. "The Major in charge needs to get his ducks in a row. I'm going to the Base Commander's staff meeting now and tell that guy what I think of his unit's performance."

I was a bit taken aback by the outburst. It was really out of character. So I made a suggestion.

"Major, before you do that, before you say anything, sit back awhile. You can never take back a word once spoken," I told him.

Later that afternoon, the Major came back from the meeting and told me to get up from my chair. He then gave me a big bear hug—something *really* out of character.

"What's that for?" I asked.

"That was excellent advice you gave me. I went to the meeting prepared to blast the Provost Marshall, but I remembered what you said. I decided to hold off. Shortly after the meeting started, the Base Commander told the Major he was sorry his wife was so ill. If I had bawled him out with everyone at the table but me knowing his wife was sick, I would have felt like a heel."

From that day, I remembered my own lesson and applied it many times during the rest of my career. Before I say anything negative to anyone or about anyone, I find out the facts and environment. I have learned to be quick to praise when it's deserved, but slow to criticize. Many times this advice has saved me from embarrassment.

San Angelo, Texas, didn't have much to offer a bachelor

officer. No excitement, little nightlife, but plenty of dates. As one of the few bachelor officers on base, I was attractive to local girls, who all wanted to marry an Air Force officer and get out of San Angelo. I dated some of the girls who worked at the local PX, but no serious romances developed. Several girls were serious about me, though, or at least the ticket out of town I could provide. Just before I left the base, one of them even proposed marriage to me. I was flattered but embarrassed, and extracted myself as diplomatically as I could.

At Goodfellow, I served both as an Aircraft Maintenance Officer and an Instructor. The job was routine, and I wanted out, but I had to have good reason to ask for a transfer. Debating my next move, I learned from a fellow officer that recruiting duty allowed him time to finish his college degree. Most recruiting offices were located in larger metropolitan areas with colleges and universities. The Air Force badly needed recruiters, so I applied and was accepted. My first post was Ashland, Kentucky, where I served as Deputy Commander of the recruiting station. My plan hit a snag, though, since Ashland was a small town with no local college.

Still, Ashland offered far more than San Angelo. I became actively involved in the community, made speeches to local organizations, and even joined the Masons, the Junior Chamber of Commerce, and the local Presbyterian Church, where I sang in the choir. Ashland was a typical company town, dominated by a large oil refinery.

A true social life was found not far away in Lexington, Kentucky, and mine was greatly enhanced by a friend and later roommate, Howard Bowles. Howard was from Berea, Kentucky. He had a tremendous personality and knew everyone in town, and most of the state as well. We often said, not completely joking, that he would be governor of Kentucky some day.

It wasn't long before the inevitable reorganization occurred, and the Ashland recruiting office was closed. I was reassigned to Lexington as Deputy Recruiting Commander for the east-

Ashland, Kentucky, summer 1948. With my friend Howard Bowles.

ern region of Kentucky.

I arrived in Lexington early in 1949 and rented a private room with its own bath in the upstairs of the home of Mrs. Minerva Sales. My rent included dinner. I was able to take several classes at the University of Kentucky to get me on my way to graduation, though that day wouldn't come until 1954 at Denver University.

In Lexington, we had a staff of 10. We all worked hard and earned our office one of the best recruiting records in the district, having met or surpassed our quotas in every category.

One of the jobs I was responsible for at the station was Aviation Cadet recruiting. At that time, the Air Force had assigned a young Major to tour the recruiting stations and motivate the officers responsible for Aviation Cadet recruiting to find more applicants. His name was Dean Hess. Dean was also a Methodist minister. When the Korean War broke out, he was sent to Korea to help train Korean pilots. Not only did Dean run the pilot school, he also started an orphan home and did considerable missionary work while in Korea. Both the

United States and Korean governments cited him for his achievements. Later, in 1957, he became famous when a movie was made about his exploits—*Battle Hymn*, starring Rock Hudson as Dean.

Dean and I became good friends in Lexington, and later in our careers we met several times. Many years later, we were both stationed at Wright-Patterson Air Force Base. Here we renewed our friendship. Dean was the Director of Public Relations for the Logistics Command. When he left, he wanted me to replace him. But with my technical training, the Commanding General didn't want to move me from my current position. Dean was a great human being, a good friend, and the most Christian man I've ever met. He continued his public service in retirement by becoming a high school teacher in a nearby school district.

Just before the Korean War broke out, early in 1950, the draft was reinstated and Lexington became an Induction Center. Those boys selected for the draft were brought into Lexington, given a physical to ensure they were qualified, and then sent to Fort Knox for processing prior to basic training. This was a busy time. As many as 500 boys passed through our doors every week.

We had no facility large enough to handle the flow, so it fell upon me as the Acting Commander (our Commander, Captain Scott Chadwick, had been transferred) to find a suitable facility and to recruit a medical staff. Lexington had few available buildings, and the one I found that would work had a reluctant owner.

I told him to name his price, and he did—about $50,000 a year. This was exorbitant rent and probably more than the building was worth. I attempted to negotiate, but the owner held to his price. I called the District Commander, Lieutenant Colonel Campbell, in Columbus, Ohio, and told him about the building and the asking price.

"Don't quibble, take it," he said.

I pressed, suggesting that we could do better.

"Take it. We don't have time for more research and negotiation. We've got to get an Induction Station started now. Hundreds of kids are coming in next week, and we have to have a place to handle them!"

When I went back to the landlord and told him I'd take it at his price, he thought I was joking. I immediately signed the lease for the building and that same day found contractors to make the necessary modifications to turn it into a proper Induction Station. We also contracted with local hotels to house

```
          HEADQUARTERS OHIO-KENTUCKY RECRUITING DISTRICT
                    U S ARMY AND U S AIR FORCE
                            2326th ASU
                    BUILDING T-225, FORT HAYES
                        COLUMBUS 18, OHIO

AIDHR-E 201.22                          12 September 1950

SUBJECT:  Letter of Appreciation


TO:       1st Lt. Louis W. Cracken
          Lexington Recruiting Main Station
          Lexington, Kentucky


          1.  I desire to express my thanks and appreciation for
your outstanding performance of the duties of Recruiting Main
Station Commander of the Lexington Recruiting Main Station,
Lexington, Kentucky, for the period 17 July 1950 to 6 September
1950.

          2.  Your personal devotion to duty is reflected by the
superior manner in which you organized and supervised the
administration of the Induction Station, and accomplished all
assigned recruiting missions thereby attaining the standing of
second place among the Honor Stations of the Ohio-Kentucky
Recruiting District for the month of August 1950, although for
part of this period you were the only officer assigned to the
Lexington Recruiting Main Station.

          3.  It is with great pleasure that I take this opportunity
to express my appreciation for a job well done. It is through
personnel such as yourself that the traditions of the military
services are upheld thus making yourself an asset to the Armed
Forces.

          4.  This letter will be made a matter of record and a
copy placed in your 201 file.


                                    Albert C. Molter
                                ALBERT C. MOLTER
                                Colonel, Inf
                                Commanding
```

and feed the draftees who began arriving within a few days.

One night I was called by the Sergeant on night duty. He had picked up some drafted men at the train station, but the train had been late, past 8 p.m., and the night manager at the hotel wouldn't feed the incoming inductees since the dining room closed at 7 p.m. I got in the car and drove down to the hotel and found him.

"These man are going to be fed even if you have to call your cooks in," I told him. "They're hungry, and I am not going to have them go to bed without eating."

The manager resisted and then called his general manager, passing the buck upstairs. I told the same thing to the general manager. He also resisted opening the restaurant.

"You have a contract with the U.S. government," I said. "Part of that contract is an agreement to take proper care of the men staying at your hotel. That includes feeding the men, so you need to feed them," I told him. "This is a serious neglect of your responsibility and could well impact any future contracts with the U.S. government."

At the time, the military carried a big stick with the local economy. The cooks were brought in and the men were fed.

After getting the Induction Station under construction, my next action was to ask a local doctor friend to supervise the physicals. The doctor found three other doctors to share the duties. For the most part, the Induction Station ran smoothly. We worked 12 and 14 hours a day moving men through the process on their way into the military, sometimes to Korea.

Most station commanders were captains, and after being a Station Commander for almost two months, I was called by the Colonel in charge of the district. A Captain had reported to the District Headquarters in Columbus, Ohio, to fill Captain Chadwick's position.

"I hesitate to send him down to Lexington," the Colonel told me, "because you're doing such a good job. However, Lexington is where he is supposed to be. Do you mind if we send him down? Or would you rather remain Commander and

I will find another job for him?"

I didn't mind and told the Colonel to go ahead and send him down here.

Captain John Dudley arrived and took over command at Lexington during the summer of 1950. We got along well and shared duties like it was more of a joint command. I was promoted to Captain shortly after Dudley arrived in Lexington. Upon my promotion, he took me out to dinner to celebrate. At the end of the evening, he handed me the bill. "Now that you're a Captain, I think you can afford it," he said.

It took me seven years to make Captain, and I felt fortunate. During peacetime, promotions were slow.

Another officer and my Deputy when I was temporary Commander was Lieutenant Harvey Beahm, a proud West Pointer who had survived the Allied invasion of Normandy. He suffered a serious head injury during the war. After a disability retirement, he died from complications from this wound. Harvey came from Salisbury, Maryland, and, years later when I was heading up the ROTC program at Maryland State, I became reacquainted with Harvey's wife and children. For four years while in Princess Anne, I helped look after them, and still exchange Christmas cards with Harvey's children today. Harvey had been a standout football player at West Point and had always hoped his son would be a good athlete. He was, in fact, and became a high school football coach and later ran a tennis club.

While in Lexington, I attended the University of Kentucky part time to build up my credits for an undergraduate degree. While there, I had the occasion to play tennis with the Assistant Athletic Director from the university. We had some tight games since my partner, Cindy, was the school's women's tennis champion. The Director introduced me to Kentucky's football coach "Bear" Bryant, who asked me if I wanted to see the football games from the field. I ended up guarding one of the gates to prevent gate-crashers. I really was not too good, since most of the time I watched the game and "Babe" Parelli, their star quarterback, run with the ball.

By far the most significant event during my time in Lexington was meeting a young lady, a student at the University of Kentucky. I became acquainted with a girl who worked for AAA, whose offices were downstairs from our recruiting office. Since I didn't know anyone in Lexington, I asked her if she knew some young ladies she thought I might like. She didn't know anyone, but she talked to a married friend of hers whose sister was going to the University of Kentucky.

Through this convoluted connection, I was fixed up on a blind date with a young lady named Peggy Johnson. Shortly before the date, Peggy's steady boyfriend called and said he would be down from New York that weekend. So she passed me on to her best friend and roommate, Marilyn Morris. Luckily, Marilyn said yes.

The campus was overcrowded with men taking advantage of the GI Bill, so the girls lived in a Quonset hut. On my way there, I remember thinking to myself as I always did just before a date with any new girl, "Is this going to be *the* girl?" For some reason, I felt that this meeting might be more serious than the others.

My first impression of Marilyn was great. She was all smiles, pleasant, easygoing, lady-like, pretty, had a wonderful personality, and made me feel comfortable immediately. She was also trusting and liked by everyone. Unfortunately, I soon found out, she was a senior and was going to graduate from the University of Kentucky with a degree in Social Work in just a few short weeks. It was May 1949.

Our first date was to a drive-in movie. Marilyn was extremely disappointed—she had expected dinner and dancing. I must have made some impression, though, because she let me get away with the drive-in date and allowed me to see her again. She even introduced me to her parents and sister, Jony, when they were in town for her graduation.

After graduation, Marilyn headed to New York for the summer to work at the Henry Street Settlement House. She had been there a month when she got a letter from me. That same week, she received a letter from her college girlfriends, including Peggy, inviting her to room with them in Lexington in the fall. Within a few days, she got a job offer to be Teenage Program Director for the YWCA in Lexington. Everything was pointing her back to Lexington.

Marilyn returned to Kentucky in the fall of 1949 to room with Peggy Johnson, Mary Rose, and Betty 'Bugs' Bartee. Each girl had a boyfriend, so many times the eight of us palled around together. For the next two years, Marilyn and I never dated exclusively, but we did date each other more than anyone else.

The war in Korea was escalating, so I volunteered for an assignment in Korea. Marilyn decided to go back to her home in New Carlisle, Ohio. For the next three years she investigated divorce cases involving children in Dayton at the Court of Domestic Relations. She decided to complete her master's degree at Case Western Reserve University in Cleveland.

I cared deeply for Marilyn, but once again I wanted to be in an active theater. I just could not see myself recruiting while the United States was fighting a war. I wrote a letter to my superior officer indicating I wanted to go. But once again, duty kept me out of the fray. The District Recruiting Commander told me I couldn't go until everything at the Induction Station was running smoothly.

Throughout the summer and into the fall, the Induction Station activities and Marilyn kept me busy. As winter drew to a close, my Commander finally released me. He printed my letter in the District Bulletin upon my departure. Finally I was accepted for duty in Korea and headed back to familiar territory.

DAILY   )
BULLETIN #38)   26 February 1951

OFFICIAL

COMBAT INFLATION BY BUYING U. S. SAVINGS BONDS.

I. TRANSFER FROM RECRUITING DUTY:
    1. The Ohio-Kentucky Recruiting District has lost a fine officer with
the departure of Captain Louis W Cracken, USAF, from the Lexington Recruiting Main
Station on 12 February 1951. Captain Cracken volunteered for duty in the "Far
East," and the United States Air Force has seen fit to honor his request.

    2. His departure is viewed with deep regret. However, we are all proud
of his desire to serve in such an active "theatre of operation."

    3. Captain Cracken wrote the following letter just prior to his depar-
ture:

            "Lt Col Allan Campbell
            Hq, Ohio-Ky Recruiting District
            2326th ASU, USA & USAF
            Bldg. T-225, Fort Hayes
            Columbus 18, Ohio

            Dear Sir:

                "I am sorry that I did not get an opportunity to
            personally say goodby to your staff and especially to you.
            I was planning to be in Columbus the latter part of the past
            week but due to personal reasons was unable to do so.

                "My duty with the Recruiting Service has been one of
            the most gratifying and enjoyable experiences I have had in
            the Service. A greater part of that is due to the fact that
            I have worked under your command and have had an opportunity
            to know you. I hope some day that I may serve under you again.

                "I will write you from the Far East and will let you
            know how I am getting along. If there is anything I can get
            for you there feel free to call upon me.

                "The very best of luck to you, Sir, in your duty
            assignment, now and in the future.

                "Please extend my farewell and best wishes to all the
            members of your staff.

                            Respectfully yours,

                            /s/ L. W. Cracken

                            L. W. CRACKEN
                            CAPT   USAF"
                                                (AIDHR-C)

II. TRANSPORTATION REQUESTS:
    1. Attention of all Recruiting Main Station Commanders, Ohio-Kentucky
Recruiting District, is directed to Changes 22, paragraph 3a (1) and paragraph 3d
of AR 55-120.

    2. Government Transportation Requests for the purpose of using taxi
service to transport individuals will be discontinued immediately.

    3. The provisions of above cited reference will be read by all Act-
ing Transportation Officers assigned the Ohio-Kentucky Recruiting District.
                                                (AIDHR-C1)

Perfecting the Business of War, Korea, 1951-1952

CHAPTER SIX

When I returned to Seoul in 1951, the city had been both bombed and fought over. Having recently been invaded by North Korea, normal commerce there had come to a halt. Most shops were closed, and many people were literally wandering about what was left of the streets looking for food and shelter. The contrast from the country I had left just four years earlier was distressing.

Much had unraveled since 1947. When I left Korea, the powers in the North and the South were busy building separate governments. U.S.-sponsored elections in South Korea in 1948, observed by the United Nations, led to the founding of the Republic of Korea in August 1948, with Sygmon Rhee as president. The North followed in September 1948 by establishing the Democratic People's Republic of Korea, with 28-year-old Kim Il-sung as its premier. On June 30, 1949, the last American troops departed Korea, leaving behind only the U.S. military advisory group to the Republic of Korea Army—in all about 500 officers and men whose mission was to complete the instruction of the South Korean military force.

President Truman wanted the troops to be just strong enough to repel any communist attack, but not strong enough to launch an attack of their own. That was the rationale behind the lack of tanks, heavy guns, and modern aircraft. We left few reinforcements behind for the forces.

Meanwhile, the Chinese Communists had pushed the nationalist Kuomintang forces across the strait to Taiwan. More than 30,000 veteran North Korean soldiers, who had fought with the Chinese there, returned home to form two divisions of the Korean People's Army in North Korea. By early June 1950, the People's Army had eight full divisions and two other divisions at half strength, all having been trained by high-ranking Soviet military advisors. The Soviets may not have had any soldiers on the front lines in Korea, but they did provide a considerable amount of firepower, including mortars, howitzers, self-propelled guns, antitank guns, and over 150 modern T-34 tanks. Facing these heavily armed veterans were half as many partially trained Republic of Korea troops, armed only with rifles and mortars. On June 25, 1950, the People's Army attacked across the 38th parallel, which started the Korean War.

The Korean War swiftly developed into a limited international war involving the United States and 19 other nations. From a general viewpoint, the Korean War was one of the byproducts of the Cold War, the global political and diplomatic struggle between the communist and non-communist systems following World War II.

The motives behind North Korea's decision to attack South Korea, however, had as much to do with internal Korean politics north and south of the 38th parallel as with the Cold War. Although encouraged and armed by both the Soviet Union and Red China, the actual invasion caught these mentors off guard. The Soviet Union, which expected a war at a later time, was busy boycotting the United Nations when the attack occurred. The communist government of China, meanwhile, was hoping to invade the island of Taiwan without having to deal with a military response from the United States.

Perfecting the Business of War, Korea, 1951-1952,

Considerable civil strife south of the 38th parallel and growing opposition to South Korea's president led the North Korean leader to believe he would be welcomed by many South Koreans as a liberator intent on reuniting Korea. Also, as a champion of Korean unification, he hoped to undermine ongoing opposition to his own regime in North Korea.

The United States was not prepared for the June 25 invasion. However, we immediately responded by sending supplies to Korea and broadening our commitment to conflict. On June 27, the UN Security Council, with the Soviet Union voluntarily absent, passed a U.S.-sponsored resolution calling for military sanctions against North Korea. Three days later, President Harry S Truman ordered combat forces stationed in Japan deployed to Korea. American and South Korean forces, and, ultimately, combat contingents from Australia, Belgium, Luxembourg, Canada, Colombia, Ethiopia, France, Great Britain, Greece, the Netherlands, New Zealand, the Philippines, South Africa, Thailand, and Turkey, along with medical units from Denmark, India, and Sweden, were placed under a unified UN command.

U.S. Commander-in-Chief of the Far East, General Douglas MacArthur, was in charge of the combined effort. The participating ground forces were grouped together in the U.S. 8th Army. The action was unique because neither the UN nor its predecessor, the League of Nations, had ever used military measures to repel an aggressor.

Even after Truman committed American ground forces to Korea, the war continued to go badly for South Korea. The North Koreans captured Seoul, the capital of South Korea, pushing the Americans and South Koreans back to a small perimeter around the southern port city of Pusan, my old stomping ground. American reinforcements held this small area, however, and on September 15, 1950, MacArthur launched a massive amphibious invasion behind enemy lines, striking at the port city of Inchon, about 25 miles southwest of Seoul. In a coordinated move, UN forces broke out of the Pusan perim-

CHAPTER SIX

eter. Very quickly, the North Koreans were forced back above the 38th parallel.

Sensing an opportunity not only to stop but also to roll back communist expansion, President Truman approved orders for UN forces to cross the 38th parallel and push the enemy above the Yalu River, which separates North Korea from China. Despite repeated warnings from the Chinese that they would enter the war if the Americans came near the Yalu, UN forces crossed into North Korea on October 7 and later captured Pyongyang, its capital city. By October 25, some advance units had reached the Yalu and come into contact with the Chinese. After hard fighting in which MacArthur's units had to fall back, the Chinese retired and MacArthur continued his offensive.

Shortly thereafter, the Chinese struck again, this time in massive numbers. UN troops, overextended, outnumbered, and ill-equipped to fight a fresh enemy in the bitter Korean winter, were soon in general retreat. On November 26, the communists cut the escape route of some 40,000 U.S. soldiers and marines in Northeast Korea, who fought their way out and were later evacuated from the port of Hungnamni. The communists reoccupied Pyongyang on December 5, and sweeping into South Korea, recaptured Seoul on January 4, 1951. Because they had overextended their supply lines and had vastly inferior firepower, they were not able to press their advantage. The communist offensive was halted by January 15 along a front far south of Seoul.

Even as the Chinese advanced southward, Truman again redefined American policy in Korea. Unwilling to engage in an all-out war with China, which could have led to a world war involving the Soviet Union and certainly would have alienated the European allies of the United States, the president abandoned the military reunification of Korea. He returned to his original goal of stopping communist aggression in South Korea.

The U.S. 8th Army took the offensive on January 25, and

the entire United Nations command mounted the powerful attack known as Operation Killer on February 21. Under pressure of superior firepower, the Chinese slowly withdrew from South Korea. Seoul fell to the UN again on March 14. By April 22, UN forces had occupied positions slightly north of the 38th parallel along a line that, with minor variations, remained stationary for the rest of the war.

I reported to duty just after the United Nations forces recaptured Seoul for the second time in March 1951. As part of the 3rd Air Force, when I arrived in Seoul I was assigned to the 67th Tactical Reconnaissance Wing. Almost immediately, though, I was sent to Japan.

"The Maintenance and Supply Group in Japan needs an aircraft maintenance officer. You're going to Japan," the Wing Commander informed me.

"I'd like to stay here with the Wing at Kimpo," I responded. Kimpo Air Base, located just south of Seoul, was the main air base in Korea. I wanted to be closer to the action. But again I heard familiar words.

"You're needed in Japan. But don't worry, your group is in the process of being transferred here. You'll be back in a few months."

The operational groups had been moved to Kimpo almost immediately after its recapture and just before my arrival. The Maintenance and Supply Group, because of all of its equipment, was the last unit moved to Kimpo. The 67th Tactical Reconnaissance Wing, based in Suwicki on the island of Kyushu, needed a staff aircraft maintenance officer in their Maintenance and Supply Group. I became their man.

The 67th Tactical Reconnaissance Wing was responsible for maintaining reconnaissance over territory occupied by the enemy. By 1951, the only enemy-occupied air bases were north of the Yalu River, in Chinese territory, and unreachable. However, Recon, as we called ourselves, had to maintain constant surveillance of inoperable bases in North Korea to ensure that the enemy did not rebuild. We also had to keep an eye on roads, railroads, and other infrastructure such as factories and dams. The 3rd Air Force was a tactical force using smaller bombers such as the B-26 and fighter-bombers. B-29s, our heavy bombers under the Strategic Command, were stationed in Japan and were responsible for strategic bombing during the Korean War.

My Commanding Officer at the Maintenance and Supply Group was Lieutenant Colonel Frank Sharp, a tough, dedicated, demanding, and competent officer. Three levels of maintenance exist in the Air Force. The first is Field Maintenance by the unit that does the flying. The second is Advanced Maintenance by a Maintenance and Supply Group of the Wing. The third is Major Air Maintenance, performed by a separate Air Depot Wing. We were in the second group.

The major aircraft serviced in my group were the RP-51, RB-26, RF-84, RF-86, and a few RF-80 reconnaissance aircraft. The P designation meant propeller-driven fighter aircraft, while the F designation indicated jet powered. B was for bomber, R was for unarmed reconnaissance. One of my primary responsibilities was the RB-26. This aircraft carried both illuminant bombs and cartridges for night photography.

The 67th Tactical Reconnaissance Wing either photographed or visually observed targets suitable for tactical missions. The 67th had both day and night capabilities. At night, we used RB-26s with either illuminant bombs or cartridges. Bombs were more powerful, but a plane could carry more cartridges. Altitude was also a factor. Fuses were set for detonation at a certain altitude, which lit up the area for observation. The mission type determined whether bombs or cartridges were used.

The Recon Wing also had a variety of cameras to choose from. One interesting camera was an image motion-compensating camera. This camera synchronized film movement with the speed of the aircraft to produce clearer photos. Korea was far from tropical, and sometimes, because of the cold weather, the cameras froze and had to be warmed to remain operational. Humidity also affected the quality of the photographs.

My group also maintained armaments and avionics, in addition to performing aircraft maintenance. In the field, the squadrons had limited maintenance support. Anything beyond field maintenance would come back to us.

Although this was an interesting and important assignment, I was not overly enthusiastic about being in Japan. I was prepared to serve a one-year tour of duty in combat, but could not see myself sitting in a rear-area in Japan for three years, which was a typical noncombat tour, while fighting was going on just across the Tsushima Strait.

Meanwhile, General MacArthur, who had publicly advocated a very aggressive military strategy that differed from the president's policies, was relieved of his command by President Truman on April 11. Under his successor, Lieutenant General Matthew Ridgway, the UN forces began to engage in a series of probing actions, basically a holding pattern around the 38th parallel. In June 1951, as this pattern began to crystallize, the Soviet delegate to the UN formally proposed discussions for a cease-fire. On July 10, 1951, following preparatory talks, representatives of the UN and communist commands began truce negotiations at Kaesông, North Korea. Talks continued intermittently for two years.

By late spring, within two months of my arrival in Japan, my entire unit was transferred to Kimpo. Even though I was at last in Korea, I still wasn't fully satisfied with my role. This was not what I had envisioned when I volunteered for active duty in Korea. I still yearned for more combat-related duties and less technical and administrative ones.

After arriving at Kimpo, I occasionally drove up to Seoul to the 3rd Air Force Headquarters. I made new friends with a number of Operations Analysis officers under the Director of Operations for the 3rd Air Force. One officer, Major Lowell Pyle, who was rather young for a Major, was leaving Korea, having completed his tour of duty, and was heading back to Wright-Patterson. He initially was a pilot in a combat unit and then switched to Operations Analysis since he had previously worked in aircraft design and development. He told me much about the types of assignments the Operations Analysis office worked on, and I relished the idea of this type of work. Here was a real opportunity to make a difference in the war effort.

More than once I let Lowell know that I wanted to be involved in work like that. Before he left, he talked to the Director of the Group, Lieutenant Colonel Young, to see if I could take over his assignment when he left. I met with Lieutenant Colonel Young and he asked 3rd Air Force Headquarters to reassign me to his Group.

Operations Analysis was a very selective operation. I was accepted over the protest of my Wing Commander and my Group Commander, neither of whom wanted me transferred. However, 3rd Air Force Headquarters had the final say. Thankfully, the Director of Operations for the Headquarters, Colonel Joe Mason, who was directly under the Air Force Commander, said he wanted me, so he got me. By the time I was assigned, Lieutenant Colonel Young had headed back to the United States. Lieutenant Colonel Ted Eklof replaced him.

Operations Analysis was responsible for analyzing current operations and providing suggestions to improve tactics and equipment. We also quantified how well or poorly these improvements actually functioned. What was extremely new about our work was the fact that it was all done in the field. Rather than waiting for results from stateside research centers like those at Wright-Patterson Air Force Base, Eglin Air Force Base, and Nellis Air Force Base, we provided analysis and the troops were able to improve their effectiveness on the spot.

Operations Analysis consisted of two groups: the supergrade scientists and engineers, civilian specialists who dealt directly with complex problems, and military officers trained in technical analysis.

Based upon my experience in research at Eglin and Wright-Patterson, and as Aircraft Maintenance Officer at Williams , I was assigned to the group as Operations Research Analyst. I eventually became the Deputy Director and ultimately Director, and was spot-promoted to Major since the position was a Lieutenant Colonel slot. The unit's headquarters was in Yokohama, where scientists took the raw data from our field office in Korea and performed complex calculations and assessments. I traveled there often to help on various projects and write a few reports myself.

My first assignment was to assess the accuracy of SHORAN, or short-range, blind bombings. Its cousin, LORAN, was long-range radar-controlled navigation. With SHORAN, bombardiers only used the radarscope and never actually saw the target, thus the name blind bombing.

This system had just been introduced in Korea, and Command wanted to determine its accuracy. My job was to perform ground reconnaissance and objectively analyze these raids to provide realistic damage estimates. I plotted locations of bomb targets as claimed by the pilots and compared these to where the bombs actually hit the earth. Most of my ground assessments were of positions near the 38th parallel in areas bombed earlier, but which our ground troops had now reoccupied. I worked with a photographer and several enlisted men, and we traveled the rough country in an adapted weapons carrier. Very near the front lines, we often faced groundfire and traversed minefields to reach the bomb sites.

During the course of making 20 to 30 assessments, we met many of the troops responsible for holding the line at the 38th parallel. We gathered the raw data, plotted sites on maps, then the scientists back in Yokohama mathematically manipulated the findings into a meaningful and statistically reliable assessment. The results indicated that the SHORAN bombings were only moderately accurate.

To help improve results, our group also tested fuses. Bombs have two fuses: one in the nose and one in the tail. The fuses determine the size of the explosion and the resulting crater. This was of particular interest for the Air Force in Korea and its active involvement in air interdiction—the bombing of railroads, roads, and bridges, as well as moving targets such as trains, trucks, and troops. Our group was interested in determining the actual effect of bombs upon targets and how to maximize the effectiveness of the fuses. Through field testing, we determined which fuses resulted in the deepest or widest craters. I also worked on temporary duty with the First Marine Air Wing in Pusan to help them optimize their air strikes.

At the time, Far East Air Force Command was worried that the number of vehicles that pilots claimed to destroy was excessive. Were they really destroying this many trucks or did they just think they were destroying them? The Director of Reconnaissance for the 3rd Air Force asked me to prepare a study. He suggested calling it Operation Cracken. I was honored, but nonetheless renamed the study Operation Cracker. During this time, I went along on several missions to observe the bombings. Because of the characteristics of the white phosphorus in the M-75 bomb, it was likely that when the bomb hit the roads, pilots thought vehicles were being destroyed because of the resulting smoke. Actually, the bombs may have hit other flammable targets, trees, or small structures, which then caused a large white cloud that the pilots thought was from exploding trucks. I was assigned the project of validating these claims.

I flew aboard several B-26s from the 67th Tactical Reconnaissance Wing to observe the bomb routes and bomb runs, and made visual and photo observations of where the bombs landed. Intelligence officers interpreted the photos. We often encountered groundfire during these missions. As a result of the studies conducted during Operation Cracker, the number of claims was reduced.

We also worked extensively to improve night photography. At the time, Intelligence was using special bombs and cartridges to illuminate the targets as they flew over in reconnaissance planes. We worked to determine which illuminating bombs and cartridges were more effective under specific conditions. I wrote one of many papers at the time on improving night photography missions. A byproduct of the study was the determination that pilots sometimes hampered the missions since they were always looking for better targets. Some pilots returned to base with too many unused bombs or cartridges. They were holding back waiting for a better target. When they exhausted their fuel or completed their mission, too often they returned to base with unexploded munitions. My recommendation, which was later adopted, was to change the mission plans to provide the pilots with more predetermined targets and fewer targets of opportunity.

Like any other modern air force, the 3rd Air Force had three primary missions: Air-to-Air, to seek and maintain air superiority; Interdiction, to attack behind the lines to paralyze the enemy's logistics; and Close Support of the ground forces. This last mission was of great interest to the Army in Korea since it was having a serious problem rooting the Chinese out of the Korean hills. Even napalm was often ineffective. The Air Force insisted it was most effective when it first, maintained air superiority and second, successfully interdicted enemy forces and supplies, thus destroying the enemy's ability to support its troops at the front. The thinking was, if the enemy can't bring ammunition or food to the front lines because the roads and bridges are bombed out, then they will be unable to complete their mission.

The terrain was hilly and wooded with few main roads. During the Korean War, the American Army was a modern army essentially fighting a third world war with an enemy who believed in attacking en masse, with no concern for losses in human life. In a preview of the Vietnam War, we eventually learned that the Chinese Army was not dependent upon logistics the same way the Americans were.

At the time, the Army often criticized the Air Force for not providing sufficient support. The Air Force set its first priority as air superiority and felt, rightfully, that unless this was obtained, its other two missions would be jeopardized. The Army, meanwhile, still needed close support, and felt it was losing many people needlessly. The top generals in Korea often discussed these parameters. It eventually fell to my Operations Analysis group to provide an objective analysis of the dispute.

As with any organization, it was a question of resources. The Air Force did not always have the resources necessary to meet the Army's requests. It had to determine what missions to fly and what objectives to meet. The Air Force looked to Operations Analysis to determine the validity of the Army's complaints. I went to the front to time how long it took for aircraft to arrive after they were called in, the length of time over target, and the effectiveness of performance. While at the front, I worked with the U.S. Army and our allies, the Korean, Greek, UK, and Turkish ground troops, to show them how to better utilize close air support. Often, scientists came over from the States to review the Korean Operations Analysis group, taking data home for further improvement. I was assigned to escort and brief them. It also fell upon me to brief the Commander of the 5th Air Force on our group's evaluations and projects.

Fighter pilots at the time complained about their A-1 CM gun sight. During sharp turns or dives, the G-forces were heavy, and the gyros couldn't keep up. The gun sights drifted, leaving them ineffective. The British had Gloster Meteor light bombers and had difficulty with stability on the tail. Under certain conditions they vibrated uncontrollably. My unit was involved in the analysis and eventual solution of both of these problems.

Another project involved ground testing to determine the lethality and the anti-personnel effects of bomb runs. We did numerous ground tests with simulated targets. We built several revetments and placed cameras in the revetments to take pictures of the action as the planes reached the targets and dropped their bombs. Our group of four officers and 20 enlisted men dug trenches and tied live goats into them to determine the effectiveness of bombs on the enemy in trenches.

I really regretted using live goats for targets, but it was the only way to validate the test. We then retreated to a nearby observation bunker where we watched a bombing run by B-26s.

We could hear the bombs coming down. It sounded like they were going to fall right on top of us.

Knowing just how inaccurate bombs could be, we were more than a little nervous.

On the Front Lines, Korea, 1951-1952

CHAPTER SEVEN

By the time I got to Korea, the war was being referred to as a police action, and we were basically in a holding pattern on the 38th parallel. That said, it was far from a quiet time at the front. Traveling in our weapons carrier, which doubled as our bunk when outfitted with cots at night, we were often caught in the cross-fire. One day, during a heavy exchange, the soldiers of the company I was staying with were busying themselves trading hand grenades with the communist forces. There was a small hill between us, and neither side could see the other. I remember thinking at the time, "What the hell are we doing, the American Army with all its tanks and planes and artillery, throwing hand grenades at the Chinese?" As I listened to explosion after explosion, I calculated the potential human loss if either side decided to take the hill.

During this particular fight, a Chinese soldier was captured. Since my interpreter could speak some Chinese, we were drafted to interrogate the prisoner. We learned quite a bit. He told us that his company commander had said that the unit was going to move back from the position the very next day.

The unit I was working had previously decided on a full attack at first light. The news from the prisoner made that attack unnecessary and may have saved many lives. As promised, the next day, the enemy unit retreated.

When we went to the front lines to try to improve the effectiveness of the American effort, we tried to stay with whatever unit had the best food—it was almost always an engineering unit. My favorite unit was a reserve engineering group from West Virginia. These men were friendly, professional, and made me proud of the American Army.

Our mission in the field was more physically demanding than I'd expected. We walked miles over rough terrain and up and down mountains, sometimes along with a column of Korean laborers carrying supplies to the front-line troops. We bedded down only when darkness fell and prevented us from continuing. The background noise—constant artillery fire punctuated by larger explosions of grenades and bombs—produced a mesmerizing exhaustion. When sleep came, it was deeper than I'd known before or since. Long after we bunked down, the gunners continued their fire into the wee hours. When the big guns exploded in the night, dust flooded the area. Our cots literally rose inches off the platform of our truck and fell back like a scene from a Warner Brothers cartoon. Unbelievably, we'd sleep through it all.

Occasionally, we had to investigate areas that couldn't be reached by vehicle. We trekked up and down hills and slept in caves being used by the front-line infantry as quarters. These were miserable quarters. Damp and cold, water dripped constantly from the cave ceilings all night long. We covered ourselves with tarps to stay as dry as possible.

One of the officers I met while on the front lines was on a board of inquiry created to review integration efforts in Korea. He was there to analyze the combat qualities of African American troops. Truman had ordered the integration of the armed forces, and Korea, a testing ground for the effort, intended to set a good example for the rest of the military. At the time,

Korea, 1951. Providing instructions on air support to the Colonel commanding the Greek contingent.

military leadership was questioning the fighting ability of these soldiers.

When Korea was first invaded, two regiments of occupation troops from Japan were among the first ordered to the peninsula—an African American regiment and a Caucasian regiment. While the Caucasian regiment had defended its territory well, the African American regiment had not. Many of its members were captured and much of its equipment was lost. This dichotomy was one of the reasons full integration of the military was being delayed.

Interestingly, the board of inquiry found that the African Americans were not poor soldiers. There was no lack of courage. Instead, findings indicated that the culture that existed at the time within the African American community resulted in a lack of confidence in the dedication of their fellow comrades. Remember, this was before leaders like Martin Luther King and groups like the Black Panthers made great strides to unite African Americans and instill pride in the culture. When night fell in Korea in 1951, these men just weren't sure the soldiers on either side of them would be there in the morning. Complicating this lack of cohesion was the fact that many African Americans felt they were fighting a "white man's war" and were frustrated with the lack of equal rights.

In the end, the board of inquiry recommended full integration, and time has proven that African American soldiers are no better or worse than their white peers.

Throughout 1951, even after the line of demarcation was again set at the 38th parallel, periods of heavy fighting continued on the ground and in the air. U.S. troop strength remained at around 260,000 men. UN forces from other nations stayed at about 35,000, and Republic of Korea forces grew from some 280,000 to about 340,000. Meanwhile, the communist forces increased from approximately 500,000 to 865,000. The enemy's armored strength also grew. Although the communists could not sustain another major offensive, their well-entrenched forces made even the UN's active defense strategy very costly.

My unit worked to help ensure Allied supremacy in the air. Air power played a key role in the war, which proved to be the first battlefield in history for supersonic jet aircraft. The Chinese had also developed into a major air power. Half of their 1,400 aircraft were Soviet-built MiG-15s, generally regarded by military experts at the time as one of the finest jet aircraft in the world. Although they operated from bases in Manchuria and seldom ventured over UN lines, the MiG-15s threatened

UN air supremacy over the so-called MiG Alley in northwest Korea. Not until the United States responded with a crash program that produced the formidable F-86 Sabres did UN forces have aircraft capable of challenging the MiG-15s. Large-scale air battles ultimately resulted in the loss of some 58 Sabres and 800 MiGs.

UN aircraft were also instrumental in their support of ground force. They destroyed Chinese supply lines and crippled North Korean airfields. The UN Air Force, retaining command of the skies despite opposition from enemy interceptors, devastated North Korean supply bases, railroads, bridges, hydroelectric plants, and industrial centers. At the same time, our naval units systematically pounded North Korean coastal points.

Even after I left the 67th Tactical Reconnaissance Wing, I worked closely with the group, particularly on air missions to observe and assess damage. Coupled with my time on the front in Operations Analysis was time at a desk writing numerous

Near the 38th parallel, summer 1951. Instructing a Korean Commander on providing air support.

reports on our findings. Many of our conclusions were highly classified. Several years later, at the Air Force's Command Staff College, I had to write a staff study and decided to use my experience in Korea as the basis. I went to the base library and asked for a copy of a report I'd written in Korea. The librarians patently refused to give me the document because I didn't have a high enough security clearance. The Commander of the college intervened on my behalf.

"Why won't you give Captain Cracken his paper?" he asked the head librarian.

"He just doesn't have the security clearance," the librarian reiterated. "This is a highly classified document."

"He wrote the damn thing. Give it to him," the Commander insisted.

The librarian finally complied.

Eventually I was moved up to Director of Research in Operations Analysis, but only after my predecessor, Lieutenant Colonel Eklof, before departing, went to bat to get me a spot promotion to Major. I was only a Captain at the time and the job called for a Lieutenant Colonel. After I left Korea, I would be a Captain again. While visiting a unit in Tegu, I found out that Captain Scott Chadwick, my former superior from my recruiting post in Lexington, was there. He was still a Captain and had known me as a First Lieutenant. I got a good chuckle from calling him up and saying, "This is Major Cracken." We had a good reunion and talked about our time together in Lexington.

Operations Analysis was a close-knit group of men. We had a continuous influx of visiting scientists observing operations and critiquing our methods and results. We often hosted the scientists and escorted them around Korea, showing them Seoul and Kimpo and explaining our air operations, tactics, and the technical aspects of our air war.

Our social life was more limited during the war than it had been during the time of the military government. When we were entertaining VIPs, we had little more to offer than a good

Korea, 1952. "Major" Cracken, after a spot promotion in the field.

game of liar's dice at the Officers' Club. Everyone played it from the General on down.

The game consisted of five dice and a cup, and followed the rules of poker. The dice were rolled, two showing and three concealed under the cup, with only the roller knowing the actual results. The player could lie high or low. He then passed the cup to the next player, who could either take the existing roll or challenge the first player. If he challenged and the roll was higher, he was out. If he challenged and the roll was lower, the first player was out. Usually no money changed hands, but we were all motivated to win. It was a relaxing change of pace from the pressures of fighting the war.

The Operations Analysis group was stationed on a former university campus in a compound along with the 3rd Air Force Headquarters and the 8th Army Headquarters. However, since

Operations Analysis was involved in a top-secret function, we had our own compound.

As the senior military officer, I was commander of our compound. The officers lived on the second floor of the building while the enlisted men bunked on the much larger first floor. The compound was less spacious and less comfortable than the house I had lived in during my time in Pusan. Officers quarters consisted of the basics—a bedroom with a chest, a cot, and a private bath. I rarely visited the enlisted men's quarters on the first floor, but once I ventured downstairs looking for one of the sergeants and saw a little Korean girl playing and running around. She appeared to be very much at home.

When I asked the Sergeant in charge what she was doing there, he was quite embarrassed. This conversation was going to take several cups of coffee.

The Sergeant explained that he often drove from our compound to 3rd Air Force Headquarters—sometimes twice a day. At one of the many destroyed buildings along the way, Korean orphans gathered to beg for food and candy from the GIs who passed by. Remembering his own children, he stopped by the BX, the base store, before these trips to get candy for the kids. He did this time and time again, and each time he noticed one cute little girl who stood off away from the rest of the group. Finally he began to stop and get out of the jeep to give her candy, but she never approached him like the other children. After a while he asked some of the *mama-sans* who she was. They said she had no one to take care of her, so he brought her to our compound. He and the rest of the enlisted men unofficially adopted her.

"We were afraid to tell you because we were afraid you would say we couldn't keep her," he told me.

At the time I discovered her, Jenny was about six years old and had been living in our compound for three or four weeks. I surprised the Sergeant when I threw in with him and agreed we should take care of her. She quickly had the run of the place. Jenny was quite shy and had a horrible scar on her neck, probably the result of one of the many bombings of Seoul during the war. I thought at the time that if I ever brought her home, cosmetic surgery could have done wonders to conceal it.

Like many of the men, I grew to love Jenny. She adopted

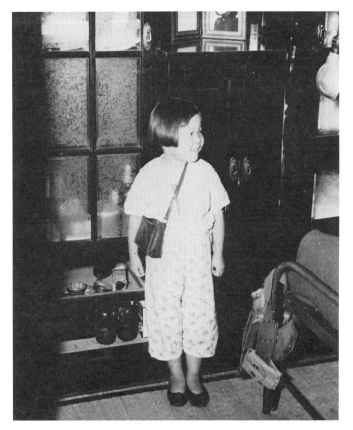

Seoul, Korea, October 1951. Jenny visits my quarters.

the Sergeant and me as her primary caretakers. When his tour was up, the new Sergeant in charge took over, but his heart wasn't in it. When my tour was up, he wasn't willing to take on the sole responsibility.

To this day, I regret the decision to leave Jenny behind, but I was a bachelor at the time and felt I couldn't handle becom-

Jenny's smile brightened our days.

ing a parent alone. Just before I left Korea, I felt I had to find a permanent home for her. I went to the Chaplain and asked him where the best place was to leave our little girl. He suggested a nearby Catholic orphanage. I talked to the Mother Superior there, and she said they would take her.

I wanted to help as much as I could before I left, so I asked the Mother Superior what they needed.

"We need blankets desperately, as well as firewood and scissors to cut their hair," she told me.

I went back to the senior Sergeant of our group and wrote out a requisition. Luckily, since our group was top secret, we got practically everything we wanted any time we wanted it, no questions asked. I told the Sergeant to get as many blankets and scissors and as much firewood as he could from the Headquarters Supply Sergeant.

"Tell him it's for a secret mission," I said.

Together with some of our airmen, we filled a two-and-a-half-ton truck with firewood, 60 or more blankets, and a dozen pairs of scissors. We drove the truck to the orphanage and gave the supplies to the Mother Superior. She was overjoyed. Though we were successful at that secret mission, we were less successful at the tough job of telling little Jenny she was

With my interpreter at the Catholic orphanage where we left Jenny.

going to the orphanage for good.

At the orphanage, she went around to each of the little children there and said, "What would you like to have my American fathers get you?" She was referring to the Sergeant and me and was trying to help out the less fortunate children. I never saw her again.

Jenny was not the only case when the duties of my command extended well beyond "the book." There were a few civil service employees in the headquarters. I had a civilian secretary, an attractive young lady who dated a helicopter pilot who was one of the many heroes of the war. His was a dangerous but dashing occupation. Late one night, very much agitated, this young lady called for my help. She and her boyfriend had argued. Later, he got drunk and broke down her door in the women's quarters. Though he had left, she was afraid he would come back, and this time there would be no door between them. I strapped on my faithful .45, got into my jeep, and drove down to her quarters. I then took her back to my quarters, gave her my bed, and slept in my sleeping bag on the floor.

I occasionally wrote to my Aunt Em and Uncle John during my stay in Korea. They always asked me if they could send me anything. Once I wrote them jokingly that I missed the lox, a Norwegian smoked salmon we both liked. Promptly I received a box from Aunt Em full of Lux soap—exactly what I didn't need. Each meal, when we walked into the mess, there were always stacks of soap, including Lux, along with cigarettes, combs, toothpaste, and toothbrushes. My buddies and I got a kick out of my care package from home.

I also wrote to Marilyn on a frequent basis and kept a picture of her in my bedroom. But I did date when I was in Korea. We worked long hours seven days a week, and R&Rs, Rest &

Lexington, Kentucky, winter 1952. Marilyn sends her love.

Recuperation leaves, were a welcome opportunity to get away from the war and recharge our batteries. I had two R&R leaves while I was in Korea. I loved skiing and went with a young lady up to an Australian R&R ski lodge in Japan at Akakura. One evening we skied away from the marked trails and got lost. It was after dark when we finally got back to the lodge, and the management was getting ready to send out a patrol. I was supposed to be the guy who knew my way around. I was trying to impress her, but I don't think I did much of a job that time.

As the war wound down, the peace negotiations seemed to never end. They were conducted in an atmosphere of mutual suspicion, and finally resulted in the settlement of all but one major issue: Communist refusal to accept the principle, adhered to by the UN, that a prisoner of war should not be returned against his will to his respective army. Negotiations broke down in October 1952 and were not resumed again until April 1953. In late spring, the two sides agreed that prisoners unwilling to return to their own countries would be placed in the custody of a neutral commission for 90 days following the signing of a truce. During this period, each nation could attempt to persuade its nationals to return home. In July 1953, the truce agreement was signed. Thus, pending ultimate settlement at the projected peace conference, the Korean War was over after more than three years of conflict. The U.S. suffered more than 50,000 casualties. South Korea sustained many more casualties, and North Korea and the Chinese sustained by far the most. The economic and social damage to both Korean nations was incalculable.

I wasn't there to see the end of the war. Near the end of my tour, I received a letter from the Assignments Officer at U.S. Air Force Headquarters in Washington indicating my next assignment was as an instructor in aircraft maintenance and avionics at Kessler Air Force Base in Biloxi, Mississippi. The Assignments Desk attempted to match openings with skills. I had been to Mississippi before, during my stint at Eglin Air

Force Base, and was not enamored with the area. I had no desire to return to the hot, humid Gulf Coast. I also wasn't thrilled about being an instructor of aircraft maintenance. I asked for an alternative assignment, and was happy when one came through as a Technical Intelligence Instructor at Lowry Air Force Base in Denver.

While I was Director of Operations Analysis, I started a tradition of giving "The Order of the Brass Turtle" to depart-

DIRECTOR OF OPERATIONS
HEADQUARTERS
FIFTH AIR FORCE
APO 970

201 - CRACKEN, Louis W. (0)   10 March 1952

SUBJECT: Recommendation for Award of the Bronze Star for
          Meritorious Service.

TO: Commanding General
         Fifth Air Force
         APO 970

    1. It is recommended that the following individual be awarded
the Bronze Star for Meritorious Service.

       CRACKEN   LOUI   WILLIAM

       Major   AO-2037320
       Director of Research
       Operations Analysis Office
       Headquarters, Fifth Air Force
       APO 970, United States Air Force
       713 Franklin Avenue, Lexington, Kentucky

    2. During the period 1 June 1951 to 1 April 1952, Major Louis
W. Cracken displayed outstanding devotion to duty in a position of
great responsibility and by his initiative and professional excellence substantially contributed to the Air Force effort against the
enemy in Korea. An urgent need existed to develop an efficient,
compact research unit to support the civilian scientists of the
Operations Analysis Office. Responsibility for organization of this
Division of the Operations Analysis Office in this theater and as a
guide to similar future units was an immediate need that had to be
met. With initiative, foresight and technical skill, Major Cracken,
as Assistant Director of Research, Operations Analysis Office,
materially assisted in meeting this challenge in an outstanding
manner. He assisted in developing an efficient and productive Research unit able to consistently obtain data in the shortest possible
time and with the highest degrees of accuracy, thereby adding substantially to the effectiveness of the Operations Analysis Office.
These research data have been invaluable to a large number of research
agencies in the ZI. In addition to his duties as Assistant Director
of Research, and since 1 March 1952, Director of Research, Operations
Analysis Office, Major Cracken has participated as Officer in Charge

ing members of our group. We took a brass turtle we bought in a local store and threaded a string through it like a medal. As officers completed their tours of duty, we hosted going-away parties and presented them with the award. To Koreans, the turtle is a sign of long life, prosperity, and good luck.

When I returned stateside in late spring of 1952, I felt lucky to be coming home whole and safe and a proud member of The Order of the Brass Turtle.

Hqs. 5th Air Force, APO 970, 201-CRACKEN, Louis W. (0), SUBJ: Recommendation for Award of the Bronze Star for Meritorious Service.

in numerous ground assessment field trips, inspecting and assessing aerial targets of Fifth Air Force and the Far East Air Force Bomber Command. When the military situation prohibited ground assessment of positions along the front lines, his voluntary accompaniment of the most advanced infantry patrols resulted in first hand evaluation of effectiveness of the Fifth Air Force close support effort. In the performance of his duties and assignments, Major Cracken has shown extraordinary facility for outstanding results. His acumen and professional excellence materially assisted his Division to undertake new techniques which have expanded the capabilities of the Operations Analysis Office and permitted that office to perform studies which, by their very nature, have substantially added to the concept of tactical air knowledge and are and will be, of invaluable service to the Air Force.

3. a. During the period cited, officer held the rank of Major.

b. No other individuals are recommended or will be recommended for the same service.

4. The entire service of the subject individual has been honorable since rendition of the service upon which this recommendation is based.

5. This recommendation is not supported by official records.

6. I have personal knowledge of the act for which this award is recommended.

7. Citation highlighting the narrative is attached.

8. a. The individual has not been awarded previously a decoration for the act described herein, nor will this act be used for any future recommendations.

b. He has not previously been awarded the Bronze Star.

1 Incl
Citation

JOE L. MASON
COLONEL, USAF
DIRECTOR OF OPERATIONS

Settling Down to Military Life, Stateside, 1952-1956

CHAPTER EIGHT

I flew from Korea to California and then to Colorado both anxious and excited to get to Lowry Air Force Base. The assignment of Technical Intelligence Instructor was a good one, and Lowry was a popular and well-run base.

At that time, there were few soldiers with combat experience returning from Korea. When I arrived, the Senior Instructor at the Intelligence School was preparing a combat training scenario for the students. The situation was a regional war, and each student was assigned a wing—bomber, fighter, recon, or transport. They were then asked to write an "Estimate of the Situation" for their wing based on the overall regional war scenario. Since the Senior Instructor, a senior Major, had considerable responsibility and didn't have the time to complete the scenario he had begun to work on, it seems I had come along at just the right time. The Senior Instructor knew I brought an experienced perspective to the job, so I was assigned, in addition to my duties as the school's Technical Intelligence Instructor, the position of Assistant Senior Instructor over several more senior Captain Instructors.

My first assignment at the school was to finish the scenario. But since I also had other responsibilities, I eventually had to write the scenario at home, where I typed late into the night, recalling years of firsthand experience gained in World War II and Korea to make the scenario as realistic and detailed as possible.

When the scenario was finally introduced for the first time, it was presented to several combined classes totaling about 70 officers. The Senior Instructor happened to be out-of-town and passed the responsibility to the Senior Class Instructor. Unfortunately, the instructor had not been briefed on the scenario. The intelligence officers in the large auditorium quickly realized he wasn't familiar enough with the material to answer their questions. Major Ellis Vander Pyl, the Deputy Director of the School and a Distinguished Service Cross winner, was called in to help; however, he was also unfamiliar with the material.

The students pressed their questions, becoming more vocal every minute, and Major Vander Pyl called me in to help. As I approached the classroom, I could hear the buzzing din of the impatient officers. As soon as I began to answer their questions, they quickly settled down to take notes. This was the beginning of a long relationship with Major Vander Pyl. Though I was there to help him out this time, he was there to support me many times in the future. From that point on we were very close.

One of my primary responsibilities at Lowry was to teach technical intelligence. This involved evaluating the enemy's equipment and technical capabilities. During World War II, for example, a complete, undamaged Zero "Zeke" Japanese fighter was captured in the Aleutians after its pilot had crash-landed the plane. We had one in Australia later. Allied engineers evaluated the fighter thoroughly to determine its strengths and weaknesses. From this evaluation, Allied pilots learned how to better combat the Zeke in the air. Additionally, based upon their evaluation, aeronautical engineers modified our Air Force and Navy fighters to better meet the challenges of the Zeke. Part of my assignment as Operations Analysis Officer in the Korean War was to perform technical intelligence estimates of the North Korean and Chinese forces. These experiences proved invaluable to me at Lowry as a teacher of technical intelligence.

With the Cold War still raging, the school was concerned with the technical capabilities of the Soviet Union and evaluated the various types of aircraft the Soviets flew in comparison to American planes. The school offered a wide variety of courses in both basic and advanced intelligence, as well as technical intelligence, photographic interpretation intelligence, radar intelligence, and some foreign language.

Though I enjoyed teaching, I still had the desire to complete my own college education. The two top colleges in the military are the Army-Navy-Air Force War College and the Industrial College of the Armed Forces. Being too junior an officer to attend either college in residence, I completed correspondence courses and graduated with honors from the Industrial College of the Armed Forces. My studies involved all aspects of support for the Operational Units—Supply, Maintenance, Transportation, Communications, etc.

While at Lowry, I was also selected to attend the Command Staff College at Maxwell Air Force Base for three months. As part of a major exercise at the school, the students were divided into four teams, and each team was required to study some aspect of the Soviet Union. My team's study was on close support, one of the major responsibilities of the Air Force and an area quite familiar to me from my work in Korea. For this simulation, however, our group was given the role of the Soviet Union. I was selected as the team's Director of Operations. After each group made its presentation, ours received the award for the best overall report.

During the evaluation of the presentation I made for my group, a friend of mine from another group came forward with some criticism. We had emphasized close support over air superiority, which my friend thought was inaccurate because air superiority is the priority of our Air Force. I listened closely to his criticism because he had plenty of firsthand knowledge. He had flown F-80s in Korea and was well-known for his antics. Once, out of ammunition and under attack by MiGs, in desperation he pulled out his .45 revolver and began to shoot at the plane. He didn't down the pilot, but he did get away.

"Please keep in mind," I told him, "in this scenario, our group took the role of the Soviets, not the Americans."

This perspective changed the emphasis, because in the Soviet Air Force, close support is paramount. The Soviet Air Forces are actually under Army control, and it follows that they are there to support the Army. From an American point of view, my friend was absolutely right, but from a Soviet point of view, he was wrong. The instructor agreed.

While at the school, we were required to write a staff study. It was here that the Commander of the school resolved my security clearance problem in the library. My staff study was graded "Outstanding" and sent to U.S. Air Force Headquarters in Washington, D.C. for study, not a normal procedure. I graduated at the top of my class. It was particularly gratifying because our position was based on four areas: faculty, fellow students, our staff study, and our grades. Lieutenant Colonel Vizi, my advisor, told me it would go on my record at U.S. Air Force Headquarters.

I was also pleased because my Senior Instructor at Lowry, Major Dan O'Brien, was a fellow classmate and my school grade was sent to the Base Commander at Lowry Air Force Base. It was a factor, I think, in my early promotion to Major, confirming my earlier spot promotion.

I was at Lowry during President Dwight Eisenhower's administration and had the opportunity to see President Eisenhower often since he used Lowry's main headquarters building as his summer White House. I was honored to be one of those asked to serve as a Duty Officer for the White House during its off hours. When I reported, I found out that meant I

SECURITY INFORMATION

RESTRICTED

UNITED STATES AIR FORCE
AIR UNIVERSITY
HEADQUARTERS
AIR COMMAND AND STAFF SCHOOL
ASSOCIATE INTELLIGENCE COURSE
Maxwell Air Force Base, Alabama

14 November 1952

MEMORANDUM FOR: Captain L. W. Cracken

SUBJECT: Staff Study Review

1. Your staff study has been reviewed by officers of the staff. Their findings have been consolidated and are set forth below. The review was conducted in order to note excellencies, defects or peculiarities of the study. Each section of the study was critiqued separately and finally the staff study was evaluated as to its overall effectiveness. The criticisms are designed to be helpful and represent the sincerest efforts and best judgment of the reviewing staff.

    a. The Problem

        Your study is limited to a manageable problem and the statement of your problem is clear.

    b. Factors Bearing on the Problem

        The facts, criteria, assumptions and definitions are considered well organized, well stated and pertinent to the problem.

        An additional fact to the effect that Operations Analysis has proved itself to be of value to a tactical air force would add to your study. This value has been brought out in your discussion, however.

    c. Discussion

        The discussion contains a brief but adequate introduction and represents a mature and sound analysis of the problem. You make excellent use of concrete examples as a basis for your conclusion.

    d. Conclusion

        Your conclusion is sound and well stated.

    e. Action Recommended

        Your recommendations are logical and complete.

    f. Tabs

        You make excellent use of tabs and they are prepared for easy reference.

    g. General Comments

        Your staff study is well organized and clearly and logically written. It represents a mature and sincere effort in the analysis of a problem of great importance to the Air Force.

        The overall evaluation of this Staff Study is considered Outstanding. Consideration will be given to the forwarding of a copy to TAC and USAF.

SECURITY INFORMATION

RESTRICTED

HUGH D. WALLACE
Colonel, USAF
Chief, Intelligence Division

was a receptionist and would be answering the phone. Still, it was interesting to see the President and his staff walk in and out and to exchange pleasantries with him. He was a very friendly man with a warm, engaging smile. When Eisenhower left in the fall, each officer who had served was given a small lighter with the White House emblem on it.

One of my most memorable experiences at Lowry was getting to meet the actor Paul Robeson. He starred in one of my favorite movies, *Sanders of the River*, but was perhaps best known for his fabulous singing voice. Robeson was a world-famous opera singer and had starred in *Othello*. He was particularly noted for his role in *Showboat* and what became his signature song, "Old Man River." Robeson was also an all-American football player from Colgate and eventually became a lawyer.

The night I met him, I had taken a young lady to dinner at Denver's Brown Hotel. As we left, we passed the all-night coffee shop on the ground floor of the hotel, and I noticed this big, husky African American man sitting by himself at the coffee bar. He looked familiar, and then it dawned on me that it was Paul Robeson. I made an excuse to my date that I wasn't feeling well, quickly took her home, and returned to the coffee shop, hoping Robeson would still be there. He was, so I introduced myself and told him I was a longtime admirer. To my great pleasure, he invited me to join him and we talked and talked into the wee hours. Robeson was not always admired in America, since he had lived in Russia for some time. Though he was not communist, he felt the Soviets treated minorities more equitably than Americans. "When I was there, I felt like everyone else," he told me that night.

Although we never communicated afterward, I felt that we were kindred spirits. When I walked away from Paul Robeson that morning and headed back to the base, I was so glad that I had taken advantage of this opportunity to meet one of my heroes. I had always been disappointed for missing my chance many years earlier with Count von Luckner.

Since I was only one semester away from completing my bachelor's degree, I took advantage of an Air Force program called "Bootstrap." At the time, the Air Force offered the op-

Settling Down to Military Life, Stateside, 1952-1956

Intelligence School at Lowry Air Force Base, fall 1953. A full social life.

portunity for officers to go on "bootstrap" for up to six months while still paying them in full. So many military men had left school to go to the war, and this allowed the Air Force to upgrade the educational level of the officer corps. I applied to the University of Denver, was accepted, and was relieved of all of my duties in order to complete my degree. It had been many years coming—with courses taken in New York City, Arizona, Kentucky, and Colorado—but I finally finished my bachelor's degree in Industrial Engineering in 1954.

While Technical Intelligence Instructor at Lowry, I lived in the Bachelor Officers Quarters. But living on the base while I was going to the University of Denver was not convenient, so I soon took a departing friend's apartment in the basement of a private home. Initially, I shared the three-bedroom place with two civilians. Split three ways, the rent was modest. The home was located adjacent to the university, enabling me to easily go back and forth to class. Not long after I moved in, the two civilians left Denver. I was concerned I would no longer be able to afford the rent, so I made a deal with the owner of the house, who was a real estate agent. I kept the apartment at my current level of payment, one-third, and on Sundays, I helped the agent hold open houses at various properties. During the six months, I actually helped sell two houses for the agent. For me at the time it was perfect. I avoided moving back to base, and even on those open house Sundays, I could study when the traffic was slow.

After I graduated from the University of Denver, I thought about a law degree. I had an attorney friend who was encouraging me in that direction. Without any preparation, I decided to take the pre-law exam at the University of Denver, an earlier equivalent of the LSAT. A short time later, the Dean of the Law School at Denver asked me to come over and talk with him. He told me my score, which was the highest of my test group, indicated an aptitude for the law, and he said that I was welcome at the University of Denver Law School any time. I never followed up on the invitation. I was in the middle of a military career and was still a Reserve Officer. At the time, my next goal was to get a regular commission.

So I returned to duty at the Intelligence School. During this time, the Air Force Academy was being built in Colorado Springs, and the Air Force needed temporary space until the academy was finished. To make room, the Intelligence School was transferred to Sheppard Air Force Base in Wichita Falls, Texas. My friend Lieutenant Colonel Vander Pyl became Director of the school at Sheppard. I had my degree now, so I was off to Texas.

While Wichita Falls is not exactly a mecca of entertainment, there were many activities for the men on base, and I remember these as good times. Sheppard was a small base and originally didn't have an officer's swimming pool. As a member of the Officers' Club Board of Directors, I petitioned for a pool, and, as a reward, I got handed the job of getting it done. I had to get the funds approved from the Air Force, design it, and, finally, supervise its construction. I also enjoyed skeet shooting, and was on the base team. Here I qualified as a sharpshooter with both .45s and carbines. I was also captain of the Intelligence School volleyball team.

The base had an Aero Club with three single-engine planes

INTELLIGENCE BRANCH
DEPARTMENT OF INTELLIGENCE TRAINING
Lowry Air Force Base
Denver, Colorado

12 November 1954

SUBJECT: Letter of Appreciation

TO: Captain Louis W Cracken
Department of Intelligence Training
Sheppard Air Force Base
Wichita Falls, Texas

1. My departure from this School cannot pass without my expressing heartfelt thanks to those like yourself whose earnest and wholehearted efforts made possible the marked advancement in the proficiency of school operations.

2. Your arrival came at a time when the school had reached its lowest ebb. Military personnel had been withdrawn for service in Korea and responsibility for the school rested largely with personnel whose knowledge of the specialty was limited to formal training. The infusion of new blood, including many officers and airmen possessing combat intelligence backgrounds, gave impetus to a revitalized program to which you personally made an outstanding contribution.

3. The rewriting or revision of all courses incorporated in our school program the lessons learned the hard way in Korea, and permitted their translation into the training of officer and airmen students. The overall effort, in which you played no minor role, has been reflected in a highly improved curriculum.

4. It became known and is now accepted as true that the prestige of the USAF was definitely enhanced by your planning and conduct of advanced reserve officer classes. These high ranking officers returned to their Reserve Centers throughout the country to stimulate a program which was hardpressed in spirit. Your instruction in the resident course for advanced officers represented the peak of effectiveness reached in this highly specialized training.

5. The opportunity of association with so fine an officer, which at the same time granted me the privilege to earn your friendship and loyalty, will be stored in the treasured memories of my long military career. This letter of appreciation is an humble and sincere expression of my gratitude.

ELLIS C VANDER PYL
LT COL   USAF
Acting Director

of its own. As a member, I could borrow a plane any time one was free. I remember many carefree hours putting holes in the sky just for fun or going down to Goodfellow Air Force Base in San Angelo to visit old buddies. One day, when I was day-dreaming while taking off, I found myself in a crosswind off the runway and heading toward a hangar. I woke up and realized that if I didn't do something quickly I would crash. I was only about 20 feet off the ground, so I dove down to five feet and picked up airspeed, then climbed and barely cleared the hangar. Instead of flying that day, I came back around and landed. I was concerned about what the Aero Club manager would say. I figured he would give me a hard time, not only for almost killing myself, but also for nearly crashing his plane.

"What do you think?" I asked him somewhat sheepishly.

"Think of what?" was his only reply.

"Didn't you see me?"

"See you what? I was having a cup of coffee."

The gods of flight smiled favorably on me that day.

It's curious that perhaps the closest I'd been to death in the Air Force was during that incident at Sheppard.

Another day I remember, an enlisted man burst into my office with the news that Lieutenant Colonel Carlson had been shot. Colonel Carlson had recently replaced Lieutenant Colonel Vander Pyl as the school's Director. I immediately went to the Director's office and found Colonel Carlson dead and Captain Marchesi, a friend of mine from Korea and an Instructor Supervisor at Sheppard, with a gaping gunshot wound to the head. Apparently, a civilian employee had suffered a nervous breakdown. The civilian, an Englishman, was an instructor of one of the school's special courses. The Air Force wanted to terminate him while he was at Lowry, but decided to give him another chance. He had recently learned that his termination was imminent. Completely out-of-control, he went to see the Director and his immediate supervisor, the two men he thought were responsible, and shot them both.

When I got there, the civilian was standing outside the office. He had dropped his gun near him on the floor. The enlisted man had already told me who was responsible for the shootings, so I immediately cornered the man and pushed him against the wall.

"I'm all right. I'm all right. I'm all right," the shooter kept insisting, obviously in a state of shock.

"I'm not concerned about you," I said. "I don't care if you're all right. Just stand right here and don't move."

I assigned several sergeants to call the Military Police, the hospital, and to guard the civilian, then I went back into the office to see what I could do. The Colonel was clearly dead, and my friend was badly wounded. Just then, another enlisted man who had some medical training entered the office. While he began trying to help my friend, I called the hospital myself for an ambulance. Then I went out and again confronted the shooter, holding him against the wall. I held him there until the Air Police arrived. When I later learned that the man had concealed another gun in his pocket, it didn't really faze me. I had never felt threatened by him. I had always felt sorry about his lack of ability to adapt, and I think he sensed that. Two surgeons from Walter Reed flew in to try to save Captain Marchesi, but he died from gunshot wounds to the head. The shooter was found not guilty by reason of insanity.

The Deputy Director, Major Cooper, now Acting Director, appointed me to accompany the body of Captain Marchesi to California for burial. At first it was an awkward situation since the family saw me as an outsider. I don't know when I've ever felt so useless, but I stayed because I had to and tried to provide whatever support the family allowed. My official duty was to give the U.S. flag to Captain Marchesi's widow. Later, the family came to me and said they didn't want me there when I first came, but they appreciated my efforts by the time I left.

After I earned my bachelor's degree, I wanted to keep going and get a master's. However, this wasn't going to happen in Wichita Falls since there were no major colleges nearby. The Air Force had some special programs available at that time, including a Master of Science in Industrial Engineering at George Washington University in Washington, D.C. I applied and was accepted for this program and was assigned there on permanent change of station for 18 months. I felt lucky to get in since only about one in every 10 officers who applied was accepted.

The objective of the program was to enable officers to study the technical environment of the Soviet Union in order to analyze strengths and weaknesses. The military rationale was to educate selective officers so they could make better target selection for strategic bombing in case of war. I was to report to Washington in June of 1955.

I made many lifelong friends at Lowry and Sheppard Air Force bases. Some were Captain Jim Fletcher, a World War II B-17 pilot in Europe who has been mentioned in several books about the European air war; Dan O'Brien, our Senior Instructor; Tony Serkadakis, an Instructor who made me an honorary Greek and changed my name to Crackadakis; and Dick Button, an Instructor.

Since returning stateside from Korea, I had visited Marilyn at her home in New Carlisle. She also came to see me once at Lowry. Based upon my experiences in Korea and my performance at the Intelligence School, I had been recommended for promotion at Lowry by Colonel Browning, the Base Commander, and listed as an "Exceptionally Well Qualified Officer." Since no more than five percent of qualified officers receive this designation, I was indeed honored. I was confirmed as a Major at Sheppard in January 1955. As far as my personal life was concerned, this promotion made me think more about getting married again and, of course, I had Marilyn in mind.

From time to time while I was at the Intelligence School, I was sent to Wright-Patterson for briefings, meetings, and seminars on technical intelligence. These trips also gave me the opportunity to see Marilyn, who was at this time finishing her master's degree in Social Work at Case Western University in Cleveland. Easter weekend of 1955, just after I received my promotion, I visited Wright-Patterson for a meeting. As usual, Marilyn came down to spend time with me. We went for a drive to a special spot of ours near a lake in New Carlisle. It was a romantic setting, and we sat in the car overlooking the lake and talked about the future.

I was more than a little gun-shy about marriage. Marilyn knew I loved her and wondered about my hesitation. I never thought I would make a good husband and was really not certain that I ever wanted to settle down. However, Marilyn had waited patiently for the past six years, and I knew it was now

AIR INTELLIGENCE BRANCH
DEPARTMENT OF INTELLIGENCE TRAINING
Sheppard Air Force Base, Texas

13 May 1955

SUBJECT: Letter of Appreciation

TO: Major Louis W. Cracken
AO 2037320

1. Upon the occasion of your departure, it is our desire to
make certain that your long and faithful service in this Department
is not ignored.

2. Therefore, we, your co-workers and friends, take this
means to express our admiration for the outstanding manner in
which you have always performed your duties. It is well known
that you were respected and well liked by the students who came
under your instruction. Upon becoming a supervisor you continued
to demonstrate outstanding ability and leadership. You have managed
to obtain and hold the highest degree of respect and spirit of friendship from your fellow instructors and supervisors.

3. So we wish to extend to you our most sincere wishes for
continued success in your future assignments and for always, good
health, good luck, and God speed!

SIGNED, SEALED, AND DELIVERED THIS 13TH DAY OF
MAY, 1955, AT SHEPPARD AIR FORCE BASE, TEXAS

FOR THE DIRECTOR:

[signatures]

or never. We had to resolve the relationship one way or another.

"Now that I'm a Major, I think we ought to go ahead and get married. What do you think?" I finally said.

"Yes. I think we should," she responded. And that was it.

New Carlisle, Ohio, at Marilyn's ancestral home, June 5, 1955. Our wedding day.

Settling Down to Military Life, Stateside, 1952-1956

We went to Marilyn's home and announced our engagement to her parents. Now we had to choose a date. Marilyn's classes were over on June 4, about the same time I was scheduled to move from Sheppard to Washington. The timing was right for an early June wedding.

I called my sister, Sara, and told her the good news. When she found out I was engaged, she told me she had always wanted to give me her first engagement ring on such an occasion. She sent me her ring, which I promptly gave to Marilyn. Today our daughter Rachel has it.

On June 5, 1955, the Morris family's Presbyterian minister married us in Marilyn's home. Marilyn's mother, Mary Van Matre Morris, called Mary Van by all her friends, made all the preparations while I was still at Sheppard and Marilyn was in Cleveland. This was somewhat in keeping with family tradition, since Mary Van had been married in her family home in Middletown, Indiana. I stayed with Marilyn's paternal grandmother until the ceremony. Jony Morris King, Marilyn's sister, was the matron of honor, and George King, Jony's husband, was the best man. They drove up from Georgia bringing along their toddler son, George Jr., "Geordie." George was an Army helicopter pilot.

After the wedding, we enjoyed a luncheon feast prepared by my mother-in-law. Then we left for Cincinnati to briefly honeymoon and buy furniture for our first apartment. We ended up buying a bedroom suite and a dining room suite that were both shipped to Washington. Since I had flown to Ohio and left my car in Washington, Marilyn's parents drove us to our new home, bringing along Marilyn's things and many wedding presents. Thus, our first married trip was from Dayton to Washington with Marilyn's parents along!

I had already selected our apartment in Washington, which was walking distance from the university. The first few nights, we slept on the floor until our furniture arrived from Ohio. It was a small place in an excellent building with a receptionist and doorman.

After a month of setting up house, Marilyn began to feel restless. Right next door was the National Red Cross Headquarters. She went there and asked if they needed any help. She then began to work full time as a caseworker at the local Red Cross, where she stayed for the duration of our tour in Washington.

After being in Washington for several months, I took Marilyn up to New York to meet my Aunt Em and Uncle John. They were very impressed with my bride, as I always have been. Though I had shied away from marriage for many years, I was a romantic at heart. Every day on the way back from school, I passed a novelty store and stopped in to buy something for Marilyn.

We both took an interest in the pigeons that lived in the city and fed them from our apartment window. Always trying to improve on things, I got a board and extended our ledge so they had a place to land. Soon we had practically all of the neighborhood pigeons at the window, and I got a call from our apartment manager. The people below us had complained to the management because they were being besieged with pigeon droppings.

The man living next door to us in Washington was from Saudi Arabia. He worked for the World Bank and had married a former American model and showgirl. We became good friends with them, which made a big difference in our social life. His position with the bank was prominent and required him to entertain many local diplomats. Often his wife, Marilyn, and I were the only Americans present at these deluxe parties.

Our own entertaining was somewhat less fancy. My statistics professor, who was much younger than I was, often came over to our apartment to play penny-ante poker with some of the other military students and me. While we may have had champagne next door, these get-togethers were more of the beer and peanuts variety.

Despite being preoccupied with studies, Marilyn and I had plenty of opportunity to visit Washington's historic sites. These day trips, which were relaxing, got me through the drier courses like statistics. I managed to graduate number two in the class right behind a friend, Bob McAllister, and right ahead of Norm Katz, one of my best friends. Grades given at the time were outstanding, satisfactory, or unsatisfactory. I received outstanding for every course but one—Linear Programming.

Finished with my master's, it was time for a new assignment. I wanted a position that involved both my intelligence background and the technical knowledge gained in Washington. The 3rd Air Force was setting up a Tactical Target Intelligence Group for Central Europe and the Soviet Union. Along with two of my classmates, Major Bob Rogers and Captain George Drury, I was assigned to the 3rd in the Intelligence Directorate. Bob and I were each assigned as Branch Chiefs, Bob as Chief of the Target Selection Branch, and I as Chief of the Target Support Branch.

The 3rd Air Force meant England. Marilyn and I were on our way to London.

The Cold War Heats Up, England, 1956-1959

CHAPTER NINE

After receiving my graduate degree, I was assigned to a NATO unit at 3rd Air Force Headquarters in South Ruislip near London. After teaching other officers the tactics of the Cold War at Intelligence School and learning some myself in Washington, I would now put these theories into practice.

In the years after World War II, many Western leaders saw the policies of the Soviet Union as a threat to world stability and peace. The spread of communist governments throughout Eastern Europe, territorial demands by the Soviets, their support of guerrilla warfare in Greece, and regional separatism in Iran appeared to many observers to be the first steps toward World War III. Such events prompted the signing of the Dunkirk Treaty in 1947 between Britain and France, pledging common defense against aggression.

Subsequent events, including the rejection of the Marshall Plan by Eastern European nations and the creation of Cominform, a European communist organization in 1947, led to the Brussels Treaty, which was signed by most Western European countries in 1948. Among the goals of this pact was the collective defense of its members. The Berlin blockade that began in March 1948 led to negotiations between Western Europe, Canada, and the United States, which resulted in the North Atlantic Treaty.

NATO, or the North Atlantic Treaty Organization, was the regional defense alliance created by the treaty signed on April 4, 1949. The original signatories were Belgium, Canada, Denmark, France, Great Britain, Iceland, Italy, Luxembourg, the Netherlands, Norway, Portugal, and the United States.

The highest authority within NATO is the North Atlantic Council, composed of permanent delegates from all member countries and headed by a Secretary General. The Military Committee, consisting of the chiefs of staff of the various

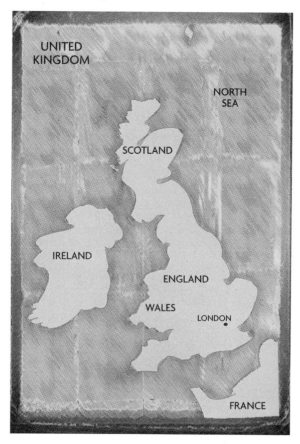

armed forces, reports to the council. Below the Military Committee are the various geographical commands: Allied Command Europe, Allied Command Atlantic, Allied Command Channel, and the Regional Planning Group for North America. These commands are in charge of deploying armed forces in their areas.

Until 1950, NATO consisted primarily of a pledge by the United States to aid its members. There was no effective machinery, however, for implementation of this pledge. The outbreak of the Korean War in June 1950 convinced the Allies that the Soviets might act against a divided Germany. The result was not only the creation of a military command system, but also the expansion of NATO. In 1952, Greece and Turkey joined the alliance, and in 1955, West Germany was accepted under a complicated arrangement prohibiting the manufacture of nuclear, biological, or chemical weapons.

As a relative newlywed, I was headed to London to be part of the NATO effort. The courses I took at George Washington University provided much of the background for this new assignment. There I had studied the international technical positions and infrastructure of other countries, particularly the Soviet Union. My position at 3rd Air Force Headquarters was Chief of the Target Support Branch. My branch's job was to provide all of the supporting maps, charts, and photography—both real and simulated—for the bombing targets, as well as this information for the routes to and from the target. My friend Bob Rogers, Chief of Target Selection, was in charge of prioritizing targets in Eastern Europe and the Soviet Union.

I worked very closely with the intelligence group at Wiesbaden, the headquarters for the U.S. Air Forces in Europe. The Chief of Intelligence for the 3rd Air Force was my immediate superior, and I had a staff of 20 to work on assigned projects.

Before I could get to work, I had to find a place to live. Bob Rogers had preceded us to England and had lived in a flat in downtown London until he was able to find a house in the

England, 1956. At home at The Thimble, North Cross, Gerrards Cross, Buckinghamshire.

suburb of Harrow, where Churchill went to school. We took the flat temporarily until we found a house in Buckinghamshire at Gerrards Cross. The house belonged to Dennis Compton, the British cricket equivalent of Babe Ruth. Compton was in South Africa with his South African wife for six months. It was a beautiful home called The Thimble, and had a thatched roof with a lovely garden in the back. To Marilyn's delight, it also came with a housekeeper and gardener.

After six months there, the Comptons returned home, so we moved to the suburb of Pinner Hill to a house called The Holt. Nicer English homes had names rather than numbers. The Holt also had a wonderful garden that backed up to a golf course. It was not unusual to go out back and pick up golf balls from errant slices. I took some golf lessons from an English pro there who had played for England during one of the

Christmas 1957. The Holt, Pinner Hill, Pinner, Middlesex, with baby Rachel.

Walker Cup tournaments. I eventually joined the Pinner Hill Golf Club as one of its few American members. I remember the club had designations for golfers with handicaps more than 12. They called us rabbits. I never reached a higher status.

During the mid-'50s, the first generation of computers was just beginning to be introduced. Up until this time, all calculations had been handled manually. My group was one of the first in the military to learn modern computing techniques such as input, programming, and output. Together with Bob Rogers, Jim Bailey, George Drury, and others, we began to computerize information on the NATO targets. This was a crucial assignment to prepare the Allied Forces for the potential threat of war.

I assembled target material folders that contained whatever information existed on each target. We kept exact duplicates in one of England's largest motion-picture studios, Denham Studios, which the Air Force leased and converted into a warehouse. If the original folders were destroyed at one of our bases in a preemptive strike, or if new units were deployed to Europe, Denham had the duplicates to ship to ensure air strike capability. Backups for targets for units in Germany were also stored in the warehouse since the units in Europe were extremely vulnerable to both air and ground attacks. The Air Force also had to be prepared to deploy air units from the United States quickly, and it was our responsibility to provide them with all necessary intelligence support.

Often no true photographs of the target existed. Relying upon information from Intelligence, we used target simulation to illustrate both the target and the terrain around the target. One method of simulation used at the time was ultrasound. Within a large tank, copper was used to simulate terrain around the target and the target itself and ultrasound echoes were recorded. We then created a simulated target and approach so the bomb crews could view the important navigation points on a screen prior to the actual bombing attack.

Bob and I made a great team. Working with him to determine the best targets and preparing the 3rd Air Force for nuclear strikes against the Soviets was one of the most efficient and effective assignments of my career. The responsibility was ominous. We were the ones who decided who got killed and who didn't. I thank God we never had to act. The result would have been horrendous.

In addition to my normal duties at South Ruislip, I was involved in the Combat Control & Command Center at Exbridge, which was set up to direct all combat operations in case of actual war. The center had a large war room with considerable statistical information and maps on the walls tracking mission status, weapons carried, and results during exercises or if a real war occurred.

I was later grateful to have become so familiar with the Combat Control & Command Center, because when a base in Aviano, Italy, opened up for rotation for fighter squadrons from the U.S., I was selected to go to Italy to help set up the Combat Operations Center there. This was a high visibility operation with the Commander General of all American Air Forces and numerous deputies in Europe leading the way. I met with four other officers to design the center and discuss what the commanders wanted to see in the program. The generals talked among themselves and left us with the responsibility of actually implementing their plans.

The Director of Operations for the base had no experience with setting up a Combat Operations Center. The senior officer in the group was a major from an air base in Germany who represented the operational side. He was a Base Operations Officer who had little knowledge of combat operations. By default, I had the most experience and took command of the group. My first order of business was to return to the 3rd Air Force in England to copy everything I could from the Combat Control & Command Center there—the directives, the boards in the war room, everything. I then returned and proceeded to duplicate them in Aviano. Aviano, in effect, became an exact clone of the Exbridge center.

Aviano is in the northeastern sector of Italy, not far from the Yugoslavian border. At the time, the U.S. was competing with the Soviet Union to maximize the threat. We tried to encircle the Soviet Union with air bases to deter war. Aviano was in a position to become a major threat because the flying time was so short between Aviano and targets near the Soviet Union's southern front. In a war, Aviano would be crucial. When I arrived, there was only a small operations office for the Italian Air Force. When we left, Aviano was a sophisticated duplicate of the Combat Control & Command Center in England. Today, Aviano is one of the most important air bases in Europe and deploys aircraft to the Middle East.

After two months, I was called back to England because a major meeting was scheduled for all of Europe at U.S. Air Force Headquarters in Wiesbaden, Germany. I represented the 3rd Air Force on the topic of targeting. Shortly thereafter, I received a Letter of Commendation from the Commanding Officer at Aviano for my work.

Headquarters
7227TH SUPPORT GROUP
United States Air Force
APO 293, US Forces

IOD   8 JAN. 1959

SUBJECT: Letter of Commendation

TO: Commander of Major Lewis W. Cracken, 34920A
          Directorate of Intelligence
          Headquarters Third Air Force
          APO 125, US Forces

    1. Major Cracken was assigned to the 7227th Support Group
on a TDY basis from 22 September 1958 to 7 November 1958 to
assist in establishing a Combat Operations Section. He was one
of five officers selected by Headquarters USAFE for this duty.
The establishment of a Wing type Combat Operations Section
operating from a completely functional Combat Operations Room
with all of the required facilities, communications, and operating procedures was an urgent operational necessity at this
station. When Major Cracken and the other team members arrived,
the Combat Operations Room consisted of four bare walls although
the majority of the communications facilities were installed
and the two Tactical Fighter Squadron's Intelligence Sections
were functioning as a combined effort.

    2. Major Cracken immediately started studying the require-
ments here and made a diligent and comprehensive review of the
Intelligence materials and procedures in effect in the two F-100
squadrons. His demonstrated knowledge of the Intelligence field
and his willingness to work hard and put in long hours to organize the new section produced outstanding results and generated
a harmonious cooperative spirit within the combined Squadron/
Group Intelligence Section. In the short time Major Cracken was
here he was able to organize an effective intelligence program
covering the requirements for our target folders, target materials, intelligence reference documents, special strike directives
as well as assisting in determining the physical facilities and
special procedures needed for the Combat Operations Room. The
thoroughness with which he screened our NATO directives resulted
in a final fix on the exact number of targets assigned to our
squadrons. This figure materially differed from that previously
considered accurate.

    3. Major Cracken's pleasant personality and his outstanding
ability to produce a spirit of cooperation among his associates
substantially contributed to the successful organization of his
section. The staff visit he made to Headquarters USAFE during

Aviano itself was just a small village, so I stayed in a hotel in a larger town about eight miles away. Every morning and evening, I traveled between the base and my hotel. On weekends, I had the opportunity to travel throughout Italy. One of my favorite side trips was to Venice, where I had the pleasure to visit the bar Hemingway frequented. Though I never met him there, I often sat in the same seat he had occupied on many occasions.

IOD, 7227th Supp Gp, Subj: Letter of Commendation (Major Lewis
W. Cracken, 34920A)

his TDY at Aviano produced excellent results and started a flow
of badly needed documents and target materials. Major Cracken's
devotion to duty, his thorough knowledge and his cooperative
attitude substantially contributed to the successful establishment of the Combat Operations Section.

CLARENCE C. McPHERSON
Colonel, USAF
Commander

2

Back at 3rd Air Force Headquarters, General Charles de
Gaulle was in the headlines again in France, and my superior,
the Director of Intelligence, called a staff meeting. The government of France was volatile at the time, and the Director
of Intelligence, Colonel Ferrill, was going to be responsible for
briefing the Commanding General on the likelihood of the
outcome of the French situation. A heated discussion ensued.
Of the nine officers in the room, everyone but me agreed that

there was no way the politicians in France would allow de Gaulle to take over. It would be too self-destructive, they maintained.

But I continued to argue. "This is bigger than any of those politicians," I said. "I think de Gaulle will be the next President of France."

I was outvoted and overruled. Colonel Ferrill went with

England, 1959. With my darling daughter.

the majority for his briefing. Nevertheless, the crisis eventually got so large that the public demanded de Gaulle's return.

Politics were fascinating to me during this dynamic time in Europe. While there, I was selected to attend a special course on International Politics at Cambridge University and spent three weeks at the school. I vividly remember a big argument I had with one of the English professors over the validity of the Nuremberg Trials. I felt that it was inevitable that these people would be tried for the high crimes they committed. The professor thought the trials were illegal since no international laws existed to use as a guide.

"You don't need laws for crimes such as these," I remember telling him. "Humanity can make its own judgment."

My engineering skills didn't get rusty in England. One important project I was assigned was to help design the Low Level Atomic Bomb Delivery System. The project, quartered at another base in Europe, involved the delivery of atomic weapons by fighters. Technology had progressed to the point at this time that small tactical nuclear weapons were feasible for delivery by artillery or fighter units. I helped develop a technique to allow the safe delivery of a bomb that wouldn't kill the pilot in the process. This work was so new that we experimented as we went. Up to this time, nuclear bombs had been dropped by strategic bombers, the B-29s and later the B-52s.

While elbow deep in this project, I got news that Marilyn would soon be delivering our first child. I returned home to be close by until the big event. On September 11, 1957, we were having dinner at the Officers' Club and planning to go to the theater. We never made it—instead Rachel Elizabeth Van Matre Cracken was born at South Ruislip Air Force Base Hospital. We were thrilled with the new member of our household. Rachel was for my mother, Elizabeth was Marilyn's mother's middle name, and Van Matre was Marilyn's mother's maiden name. Rachel was a beautiful baby. Our nickname for her was "Pumpkin," which I still sometimes use privately.

Marilyn's parents had flown to England to help, arriving within a few days of Rachel's birth. We also hired a German girl, Eva, as an au pair. Eva had worked with several military families. Her current host family was returning to the States, and without a new one, she would have to return to Germany. So our timing was perfect. Eva stayed with us for the remaining two years of our tour in England. When we left, she went to work for General Disasway, Commander in Chief of U.S. Air Forces in Europe. Later, she married one of the General's aides.

Marilyn and I visited much of Western Europe while stationed in England. We went to Paris several times. On one trip with several other military officers and their wives, we went to several nightclubs. At the first nightclub, the seductive singer chose me from the audience to come up onstage and dance with her. We later moved on to a second nightclub, where the singer also looked to the audience for someone to serenade. To my group's surprise, she also chose me. The third nightclub had an elaborate stage with a winding staircase up to a boudoir. The beautiful entertainer came to the audience and took me by the hand to lead me up the stairs. My group, understandably, roared with laughter. The young lady was completely dismayed.

While we had gone to Paris to partake of the wonderful French food, we most enjoyed a stop for lunch at the American Embassy. The cafeteria there served good old American hamburgers and milkshakes.

We traveled all over England, visiting historic locales such as Stratford-on-Avon, Cornwall, Devon, and Scotland. Being an English history buff, I made the best of it, seeing as many historical sites as I could. We also managed to see my Aunt Em and Uncle John several times during this period, since they always came to Europe for the summer.

An enjoyable social occasion was to attend the Changing of the Guard in London, which happens in June as part of the official celebration of the Queen's birthday. There are six formal rehearsals of the Changing of the Guard before the actual event. Social position in England determines which rehearsal you are invited to attend. The first year, Marilyn and I were not invited at all. By the time we left England, we had attended the third rehearsal.

When I went to England, I was still a reserve officer. While there, I was commissioned as a regular officer, a designation generally limited to West Point graduates. This had long been my goal. A regular commission in the military required approval by the Senate for each individual selected, in the same manner as judges. Since the majority of the armed forces at that time were reserve, the Air Force commanders decided that they needed a few more regular officers for stability. They selected a handful of reserve officers to upgrade to regular status, and I was one of the lucky few.

My assignment in England was a designated tour of three years. Near the end of the third year, I began to anticipate my next assignment, thinking about where I would like to go. My best friends there, Bob Rogers and George Drury, and I discussed opportunities to get doctorate degrees. We all decided to apply for ROTC duty since we would be assigned to universities where we could pursue our studies. Only a limited number of universities in the United States had Air Force ROTC programs. Bob Rogers was assigned to Princeton University and George Drury was assigned to New York University.

I was assigned to the University of Maryland. Though less prestigious than the universities my friends were headed to, I was excited about the assignment and the opportunity to work on my doctorate degree. I was already acquainted with the University of Maryland system. While in England I became a friend of the Dean of the University of Maryland program there. He offered me an assistant professorship at the school in England where I taught industrial management courses in the evenings.

Our family, now numbering three, headed back across the Atlantic to Maryland.

Training Future Soldiers, Maryland, 1959-1963

CHAPTER TEN

I arrived in College Park, Maryland, expecting to be an instructor in an Air Force ROTC unit at the University of Maryland, but Colonel Aylsworth, the professor of Aerospace Science and the Director of the University of Maryland ROTC detachment, decided to assign me to another campus—Maryland State College. Located on the eastern shore of Maryland on the Chesapeake Bay near Princess Anne, and just a few miles from Salisbury, the largest city in the area, Maryland State College was the "black school" of the University of Maryland System. When I arrived, only three out of 60 professors were white, and although white students were permitted to apply, they represented less than one percent of the student body.

Colonel Aylsworth explained that my broad background and Marilyn's expertise in social work made us a better fit for the satellite campus than any other candidate he had at the time. These were volatile times in the South, and the civil rights movement was just beginning its rise.

The Maryland State tour began during the fall semester of 1959. I was head of the Air Force detachment at the college and was given the title of Associate Professor of Aerospace Science. The Air Force ROTC (AFROTC) officers at the university were considered faculty. My superior, Colonel Aylsworth, was also considered a full professor by the university. I had another officer working with me as well as two enlisted men. The fifth member of our department was a student secretary. My class load included teaching juniors and seniors courses in Air Force history, leadership, navigation, avionics, aircraft maintenance, and other related subjects.

The college had a difficult time attracting white faculty members. In the four years I was at Maryland State, only four or five white applicants were invited to visit the campus. When this did occur, Dr. John Williams, Maryland State's President, would call me at home and say, "I'm getting an applicant in here, a white applicant. I would like you to be his escort." I would then host the applicant, providing a tour of the facilities and potential housing. Eventually, two applicants accepted positions. One was a music teacher. The other, a native of France, taught French.

Initially, I was somewhat disappointed with the appointment, not because this was a "black college," but because Maryland State did not offer postgraduate degrees. After all, one of the reasons I chose the AFROTC assignment was for the opportunity to obtain a doctorate degree. Once again in my career, I hadn't gotten the assignment I'd wanted. But as in every other instance, I would find opportunity to learn and benefit from my experiences.

The AFROTC program had two sections—the first two years were mandatory for all male University of Maryland students. The second two years were elective. We selected those students we felt best qualified and encouraged them to apply for the advanced AFROTC. Maryland State AFROTC had an enrollment of approximately 600 basic cadets. Of those, only 25 applied and were accepted for advanced training for the last two years. Upon graduation, they earned a commission in the reserves and went on to active duty in the Air Force. Since the ROTC program was only for boys, we had an auxiliary program for coeds called Angel-Flight. In their quasi-ROTC blue uniforms, they served as hostesses at many ROTC func-

Marilyn and Bob Ford, a favorite student and his bride.

tions, including drill team exhibitions and rifle competitions.

Before graduation, I could nominate any student I thought was exceptionally qualified for a regular commission. A board consisting of ROTC officers decided if the student was qualified and, if so, recommended the student to the Air Force. In the four years I was at Maryland State, I only nominated one student as exceptionally qualified—Bob Ford, the Cadet Colonel and the Commander of the Cadet Corps. He was confirmed by the board and accepted by the Air Force for a regular commission. Marilyn and I both greatly admired this young man.

Dr. John Williams, Maryland State College's distinguished President.

Marilyn practically adopted him and introduced him to a young lady, also named Marilyn. The two eventually married, and Bob went on to do well in the military.

Racial tension in Maryland was a reality that had to be considered. Maryland State avoided the race riots that characterized those times, but one time I did have to intervene on behalf of some students who were arrested in town after an incident. It was a minor charge; they had parked in the wrong parking place. The students gave the sheriff a hard time, talking back and insisting they could park wherever they wanted. The sheriff promptly put them in jail.

The story quickly spread, and the school was in an uproar. Some of the more radical students started putting together a group to go to town and break the students out of jail. The largely white, strictly segregated town (many members of which had never been very happy with having a "black school" such a short distance away), would have retaliated in an instant. A major confrontation was brewing. Dr. Williams asked me to intervene, so I had a long talk with the sheriff. He, too, was alarmed at the prospect and danger of a riot. Finally, he agreed to let the students go free with a warning.

We lived in Princess Anne, a predominantly white community just a short distance from the college. Few people if any in the town had contact with the college, or any African Americans for that matter. Unlike most of the townspeople, we had many African American friends. Marilyn invited them to our home to play bridge. Her regular bridge group included Mrs. Williams, the president's wife, the University Registrar, and several female faculty members. All happened to be African American. We never thought a thing about it.

The Williams were some of the closest friends we have had. Marilyn and I spent many evenings in the recreation room in Dr. Williams' basement eating hard-shell crabs from Chesapeake Bay by the barrel. Dr. Williams was a big, husky man. In his youth, he was an All-American football player and one of the top African American athletes in the country. When our son, John, was born on October 15, 1960, Dr. John Williams was one of his many namesakes. John Robert William Cracken was also named for Marilyn's father, John Robert Morris, and for John Viscardi, my uncle. William was my father's name. The day after John was born, the announcer at the Maryland

State football game broadcast the news to a packed stadium, which erupted with cheers.

One of the numerous faculty boards I sat on at Maryland State was the disciplinary board. I once had to pass judgment on one of my favorite students, a football player who made good grades. He had broken into the cafeteria after-hours with several of his friends. The boys were hungry and cooked them-

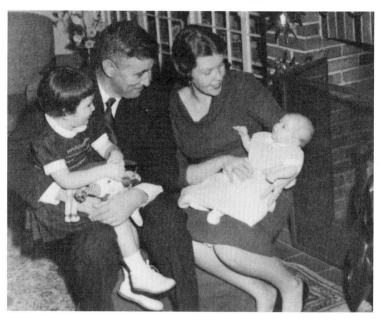

Princess Anne, Maryland, 1960. Our new addition.

selves some steak and eggs. The football coach was afraid all of these students, including his prized player, would be expelled. At the time, Maryland State had an excellent football team. They rarely lost more than one or two games in a season, and sent numerous players to the NFL over the years. I occasionally served as the announcer for football games at Maryland State and was pretty good friends with the coach, so he brought his player to my home to see me before the board convened, thinking I would be empathetic.

What the coach and his player didn't know is just how well I understood the situation. This was the second time in my life I was asked to judge young boys who had stolen food because they were hungry. The coach and the accused player didn't know that, based on my past experiences, I had already decided to vote for a mild punishment, not expulsion.

A week before the board was to meet on this matter, Dr. William's wife died of cancer. Because of the timing of the funeral, the disciplinary board never met to judge the hungry students. Eventually, the incident blew over.

Mrs. William's death was a great loss to the whole school community. Dr. Williams had asked me to participate in the funeral ceremony with a select group of my cadets. In the gym, in a closed casket ceremony, these cadets in their formal uniforms stood at attention on either side of the casket. The honor guard pointed its rifles toward the ground. Rifles reversed, a British custom, is a sign of honor. This military ceremony was not entirely appropriate to the United States, but since I had no experience in the correct procedure, I improvised. Dr. Williams requested the ceremony, so I obliged, hoping to ease his grief in some way. Later, shortly before I left Maryland State, I suggested the campus plant a tree in Mrs. Williams' honor. During an informal ceremony, Dr. Williams planted the tree and placed a plaque at its base. When Dr. Williams died, a tree was also planted on campus in his honor.

One of the most important roles I had at the college was to plan and lead the annual celebration of Armed Forces Day. This was perhaps the biggest celebration day of the year for Maryland State. The entire college closed down, put on a parade, and spotlighted ROTC for the whole day. The Air Force Drum and Bugle Corps routinely attended our ceremonies. The University of Maryland band and drill teams, as well as bands from the entire multistate area, also took part in the festivities. Usually we invited a general from the Pentagon to provide the keynote speech. It took most of the year for us to organize the event.

We went all out because I felt my superior at the University of Maryland, the District Commander, a full Colonel, and the Brigadier General in charge of all of the AFROTC programs, General Lindley, were all judging us. The success of each year's Armed Forces Day left a strong impression with them. General Lindley later became a friend. He retired to San Antonio and eventually joined me on the Board of the Victoria Courts Child Care Center, a government-sponsored child-care center, the largest in San Antonio, which Marilyn and I have been active in over the years.

Perhaps the most memorable Armed Forces Day celebration was one that included the elite U.S. Air Force Drum and Bugle Corps. As they marched down the football field, they were so impressive, completely obscuring the grass field with their numbers. I sat on the sidelines on the football bench with my son, John, who was just a toddler at the time. As the Corps approached us, John ran onto the field and into the middle of the performers. They expertly side-stepped him until I could go out and pick him up, returning him safely to the sidelines. The crowd roared with approval.

Armed Forces Day, 1963. Presenting the Outstanding ROTC Cadet Award.

While at Maryland State, I became a certified instructor for the National Rifle Association in both the pistol and rifle. An instructor certification is the highest designation the NRA gives. I later created a rifle range and started a rifle team for the school. Chess was another of my interests, so I also founded and sponsored a school chess club.

While at Maryland State, I went to U.S. Air Force Head-

Training Future Soldiers, Maryland, 1959-1963

Armed Forces Day, 1963. Receiving the President's Cup.

quarters and requested a salvaged F-86 jet fighter for the college campus. When the request was approved, I went to Dover Air Force Base, my support base, and, with several mechanics from the base, brought back a dissembled plane and reassembled it on campus in honor of the Air Force ROTC. The local American Legion was upset that the plane was brought back for the school and not for the town. So I called Air Force Headquarters, and when it was approved, went back to Dover Air Force Base for support. Eventually we set up another plane outside the American Legion Post. This was just another symptom of the poor relationship that existed between the white community and the college.

I was proud of the contributions I made to Maryland State and honored that I was well received there. During my tenure, I was the only white faculty member to earn the Outstanding Faculty Member of the Year award, the President's Cup, and the Faculty Cup. I was also asked to crown the queen at homecoming. Truly, I was overwhelmed by the attention. In the 1962 yearbook, there was a full page called the Colonel's Page about

June 1963. Receiving the Outstanding Faculty Member Award.

my family and me. And in 1963, I was particularly proud that the yearbook was dedicated to me. The AFROTC cadets also inscribed the cover of the book with a special dedication.

Usually tours are three years in length, but Dr. Williams had requested and was given approval to extend my stay by a year. Staying on another year was a good thing for Marilyn, who had been asked by the Somerset County Welfare Department to do casework. After John was a year old, she started working for the county on a part-time basis, three days a week. Felicia, our maid, was a good nanny for the children. Marilyn's job quickly extended to five days a week, and Felicia's job as

The   C
       O
       L
       O
       N
       E
       L'
       S

P
A
G
E

Mrs. Cracken, Rachel, Colonel Cracken, Billy.

Dedication

Because, by his alertness and sensitivity to the ideals and goals of both his students and his colleagues, by his imparting the message through precept and example that the good life and the fair life are one, by his insistence upon serving the common welfare: because by these tokens he has contributed immeasurably to making the life at Maryland State College a good life for four dedicated, busy years; in sum, because he is a good man who does good things from which we have all benefited, we dedicate this issue of THE HAWK to

COLONEL LOUIS W. CRACKEN

THE HAWK

1963

TO LIEUTENANT COLONEL LOUIS WILLIAM CRACKEN
Teacher, Soldier, Gentleman, Friend
FROM THE CADET OFFICERS
OF THE MARYLAND STATE COLLEGE AIR FORCE ROTC IN
GRATITUDE FOR HIS SERVICE TO THE CORPS, 1959-1963

The Maryland State yearbook, 1963. A special dedication from my cadets.

cook, nanny, and housekeeper also became full-time. Felicia was an excellent cook who made a wonderful sweet potato pie. We missed her dearly when we moved.

Princess Anne, Maryland, 1961. John and our housekeeper Felicia Gayle.

A lady we hired as John's temporary nanny came to me in tears after her brother, a gardener, had been denied his check at the local welfare office. He had not found work that month and welfare was the only income he had. I asked her to have him come to our house so I could go with him down to the office. It was during the week, and I was in full uniform. We went to the office of the Director, and I asked him why the man had not received his check. The Director said he had asked him if he had looked for a job that month, as the law required, and the man had said no. So I looked at him and asked him, "Did you look for a job this month?" He said, "Yes, sir, I did."

"Now give him his check," I told the Director.

To my surprise, he reached into his desk drawer and handed over the check. It was the fastest bureaucratic reaction I'd ever seen!

We left behind many good friends in Maryland. One of them was Head of the Department of Music and an excellent

LAST NAME—FIRST NAME—MIDDLE INITIAL			ACTIVE DUTY GRADE	AFSN
CRACKEN, LOUIS N			LT. COL.	34920A

(CHECK APPROPRIATE BLOCK AND COMPLETE AS APPLICABLE)

☐ SUPPLEMENTAL SHEET TO RATING FORM WHICH COVERS THE FOLLOWING PERIOD OF REPORT		☒ LETTER OF EVALUATION COVERING THE FOLLOWING PERIOD OF OBSERVATION	
FROM	TO	FROM **18 March 1962**	TO **17 March 1963**

Precede comments by appropriate data, i.e. section continuation, indorsement continuation, additional indorsement, etc. Follow comments by the authentication to include: name, grade, AFSN, organization, duty title, date and signature.

Lieutenant Colonel Louis N. Cracken, AFSN 34920A, has informed me that he will complete his tour of duty at Maryland State College at the close of the present school year. I wish to take this opportunity to tell you about the impact of his administration of the College Unit of the Air Force Reserve Officers Training Corps upon the institution and its student body and the community in which we live.

Maryland State College has not had an officer superior to Colonel Cracken. If he has any serious weakness, no one has been able to discover it. His thoroughly analytical mind, his attention to the most minute details in his day-to-day performance, his exacting standards for students, his excellent discipline, have all worked together to make him an example for his colleagues to emulate.

Because of our high regard for his professional competence, Colonel Cracken has been a member of virtually every important administrative committee in our organization, among them the Administrative Council, which has to do with the overall administration of the College, and the Student Life Committee, which is charged with matters concerning student life and discipline. We shall miss Colonel Cracken's sound judgment on these committees, as well as his thinking and actions in matters strictly educational.

Any consideration of the personality of Colonel Cracken would have to include his honesty, integrity, loyalty, and concern for the welfare of the students under his supervision. He is highly respected by faculty, staff, and students for these qualities and in the exhibition of them he has brought great credit to the College and the community.

Without fanfare or publicity, solely as a good citizen and worker in the community, Colonel Cracken has been able to bring influential persons to the College who would not have come without the influence of his easy manner of developing friends of the institution. It is my personal feeling that in integration of the races in the local community, he has been a great force for developing respect for the College, to so great an extent that we now have a concerted movement by the local community to bring the College program to the attention of the whole Eastern Shore.

Let me say finally that Colonel Cracken is a man who is always willing to go cheerfully beyond the last mile for the welfare of the institution and the community with which he is concerned.

J. T. Williams
President
Maryland State College

AF FORM 77a JUN 61   PREVIOUS EDITIONS OF THIS FORM ARE OBSOLETE AND REPLACES AF707A MAY 60 WHICH IS OBSOLETE   U.S. GOVERNMENT PRINTING OFFICE : 1961 O—613945   SUPPLEMENTAL SHEET TO AF FORMS 75, 77, 707 AND 475.

pianist. One Christmas, Rachel was given a miniature piano. He came over and played the most beautiful music you could imagine on that toy piano. Later, President Kennedy appointed him to the National Arts Commission. Our closest friends were Omro and Florence Todd. He was the minister for the local Methodist Church and christened both of our children while we were there. The Todd's son, Mark, and Rachel were inseparable companions. We still see the Todds occasionally.

MARYLAND STATE COLLEGE
DIVISION OF UNIVERSITY OF MARYLAND
AT PRINCESS ANNE
PRINCESS ANNE, MARYLAND

DEPARTMENT OF SOCIAL SCIENCES

June 7, 1963

Colonel Louis W. Cracken
Campus

Dear Bill:

I understand that today you are signing out, terminating
your official tour of duty at the College, prior to assignment
in Norway. I trust that your leaving, however, will not end
the excellent relation you established in rendering significant
and outstanding service to College and community. Indeed, I do
hope and trust that some day you will revisit us, possibly returning in another capacity to continue your able services.

Nevertheless, I trust that you will take with you upon
leave a knowledge of our deep appreciation and high esteem.
I need not cite here the many times we called upon you to help
us out in the instructional program when emergencies or unfor-
seen circumstances arose. I recall particularly the course in
European history you taught for us for an entire semester when
one of our staff members became disabled. There were also many
times in which we called upon you to serve as a special guest
lecturer in several classes. I take the time now to thank you,
again and again. I realize, ofcourse, that my deep and sincere
thanks are not an adequate reward for your sacrifices and services.

Moreover, I have found you to be personally a very fine
person-- and a hell of a swell guy.

With every best wish for you and family, I am

Cordially,

W. A. Low
Prof & Head

Omro retired from the church and became a professor in the
Social Sciences.

In 1962, I was promoted to Lieutenant Colonel. In the
summer of 1963, I was assigned as Vice-Commander of training officers of an Air Force ROTC summer camp at Lockburne
Air Force Base in Columbus, Ohio. All advanced cadets in
their final year were required to attend a summer camp to receive commissions. The base was a Strategic Air Command

Base. The Strategic Air Command was considered the elite command in the Air Force. Its mission was strategic bombing with nuclear weapons, the major U.S. deterrent to World War III. Its commander was the most respected and feared General in the Air Force, General LeMay. He later became Chief of Staff of the U.S. Air Force. I was a little concerned about being assigned to a Strategic Air Command Base out of a comparatively loose Air Force ROTC Military Unit. However, I enjoyed the assignment and found the Strategic Air Command officers surprisingly human.

By the spring of 1963, it was time to move on. I had two choices—to take whatever the assignment group gave me, or to go to Washington where the assignments were made and explore what was available. I was anxious to return overseas and so was Marilyn.

I remember asking directly, "What's available overseas for a Lieutenant Colonel with my specialty?" Since I had considerable intelligence experience and some planning background by this time, I was asked if I wanted to go to Norway to NATO.

It didn't take more than a minute to decide. "I'll take it," I said. We were on our way to Oslo.

NATO on the Russian Front, Norway, 1963-1966

CHAPTER ELEVEN

I arrived in Oslo at 2 a.m. with Marilyn, young Rachel, and John in tow. Despite the late hour, an American officer from the American detachment in NATO, Lieutenant Colonel Jack Webster, who had been selected as our escort officer, was there to meet us. He and his wife took us to our hotel and, on the way, learned that we hadn't eaten since early that day. Jack asked the hotel manager if he could provide any food. The kitchen had long since closed, so we sat talking with the Websters in the lounge for a few minutes, expecting to go to bed hungry. Then in walked the hotel manager with a huge platter—an entire smoked salmon complete with all of the trimmings. The six of us sat talking and eating salmon for more than an hour before Marilyn and I took the children up to bed.

The next day, we moved into our new home. I had been fortunate before we left the States to correspond with Lieutenant Colonel Frazier, who I would replace in Norway. He had rented a home from a Norwegian and offered the lease to us. The owner of the house was Mr. Scotvedt. His family owned a printing press factory as well as other business and

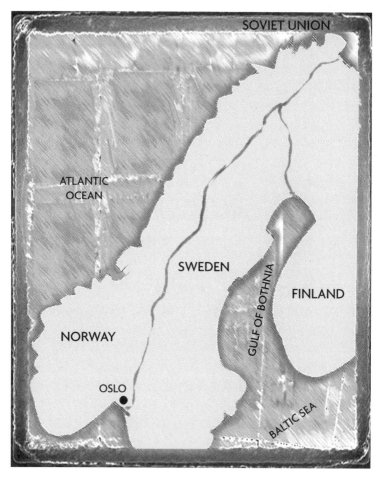

real-estate interests in Norway. He lived in his family home on the water directly below the house we rented. The home we occupied was originally a hunting lodge that had been expanded. Mr. Scotvedt had lived there until his father died. Located on top of a steep hill, it had a breathtaking view of Oslo and the surrounding fiords. The owner was quite kind to us and even loaned me his British MG until my own Volkswagen station wagon arrived from Germany.

Mr. Scotvedt was a Major in the Norwegian Army reserves when the Germans invaded Norway during World War II. He told me how he and others shot at the German paratroopers as

Oslo, 1963. Rachel, John, and Marilyn.

told me how he and others shot at the German paratroopers as they landed at the Oslo airport. "We were just outnumbered," he explained. "We fought until we were surrounded, then we had to surrender. What else could we do?"

Mr. Scotvedt's wife was a German countess, so after the occupation, he and the Germans got along well.

Norway has always been a strategic location for Northern Europe. After NATO was formed, Allied Forces Northern Europe (AFNORTH) made its headquarters in Oslo. NATO is divided into several major divisions: AFNORTH, covering the northern part of Europe; AFCENT, covering Central Europe and based in Paris; and AFSOUTH, covering the southern sector and headquartered in Naples. There is also a Navy unit based in the United Kingdom. Technically, the entire American Atlantic fleet is considered part of the NATO forces. In the '60s when I was there, AFNORTH covered Norway,

Denmark, Iceland, Greenland, the United Kingdom, and parts of northern Germany. The staff of the Oslo headquarters consisted of Norwegians, Danes, British, Americans, and Germans, and included all branches of the military.

AFNORTH was a critical area for the defense of Europe because of its proximity to the Soviet Union and its Northern fleet. In addition, the Soviet surface fleets were based in the Baltic Sea, in the Black Sea, and in the Pacific. The Black Sea fleet could easily be stopped because Turkey and the Bosphorus provided the only outlet to the Mediterranean. The Pacific fleet was outnumbered and posed no significant threat. The Baltic fleet could not quickly reach the Atlantic because it could not maneuver past the straits between Denmark and Norway.

More critical and more menacing than the Soviet surface fleet was its nuclear submarine fleet, based in the Murmansk area (the Northern Fleet). Soviet military doctrine was heavily oriented toward submarine warfare, created to disrupt the shipping lanes between the United States and Europe and prevent reinforcement of the American forces on the European continent. These nuclear subs had the capability to launch missiles with a range of up to 2,000 miles. The majority of the submarines were based at Murmansk and had to circumvent Norway before they would be a threat in the North Atlantic. Strong NATO Navy and Air Force bases in Greenland, Iceland, Scotland, and Norway could interdict Soviet submarines. However, Soviet forces on any of those points would threaten our strategy. As the most vulnerable, Norway was the linchpin of the defensive strategy.

The logical objective of the Soviet Union was to occupy as much of the Norwegian coast as possible to provide coverage and ports for its submarines to penetrate the North Atlantic. AFNORTH's defensive priority was to deny the Soviets this access. Part of our job in Intelligence was to discern the strategy the Soviets would use to occupy Norway. One of our major challenges was determining the reaction of Finland and

Sweden, two neutral countries, if the Soviets invaded.

The Norwegians had a small armed force at the time on active duty and a draft to augment their forces. We made intricate plans for bringing in American and British troops, but we couldn't have nuclear weapons or Allied forces in Norway unless there was an enhanced threat. The Norwegians were far too sensitive to antagonize the Russians.

I was first assigned the position of Director of Intelligence for Plans, Security, and Technical Intelligence. Mine was the number three slot in Intelligence in Northern Europe. The number two slot was allocated to a U.S. Navy officer as Executive Officer. Commander Ben Johnson, a Navy aviator filled that position. There were three other Directorates—Army, Navy, and Air Force. These Directorates maintained the Status of Soviet Focus and the estimates of their threats.

The officer who was one of my closest friends at the time was Wing Commander Frank Campbell of the Royal Air Force, a fine and dedicated officer. Our families became close during my time in Norway. When I was in England attending the War College, Frank died of a heart attack in Norway. I escorted his children, who were in boarding school in England, back to Norway. His wife selected six officers to be pallbearers at his funeral, and I was proud to be one of them.

My first superior was a Danish officer, Assistant Chief of Staff, Intelligence, Colonel Engholm, a talented officer who had served in the French Foreign Legion. He sang many Foreign Legion songs, played the piano superbly, and was just my type of guy. I had always been intrigued by the Foreign Legion, having read *Beau Gest* and all of its sequels when I was a young man. I had also seen the movie starring Gary Cooper. Upon his return to Denmark, Colonel Engholm became Commandant of a Danish Base, and I visited him there several times.

During my tour, Sir Robert Bray, a full General from Great Britain, commanded AFNORTH. His Chief-of-Staff was a British Major General. The deputy commander position was

Telephone:
OSLO 55 66 90

HEADQUARTERS
ALLIED FORCES NORTHERN EUROPE
Kolsås, Norway

2 April 1965

Dear Joyce, Michael, David and Lindsey,

May I take this means as a friend and colleague of
Frank's to express again, to all of you, the deep affection
and respect that I, and all of the people in this Command,
had for him; and the deep individual sense of loss we all
feel.

Frank's position as Chief of Air Intelligence for this
Command was extremely important, carrying with it great
responsibilities not only towards Great Britain but NATO as
well. The work he accomplished here will have its effect
for years to come in strengthening the military position of
the Western Alliance in the North. Frank's position alone
warranted the respect of the officers and other ranks; his
professional competence, intelligence, sincerity and dedication transformed this respect into devotion and affection,
given only to a select few who are lucky to have the rare
qualities of outstanding leadership, character and ability.

I have had the privilege and honour of working with
Frank on many plans and projects he initiated and implemented
within this Command, and in some cases within the whole of
the Allied Command Europe. I have noted the ever increasing
responsibilities placed on him by our Commander-in-Chief, and
the respect with which his opinion was heard and accepted.
There is no doubt in my mind, and that of his other friends,
that he was one of the most outstanding officers ever assigned
to this multi-nation and multi-service Headquarters. We feel
that what he accomplished here was of extreme value to the
whole of the free world, and of which you his family, his
country and his service can be justly proud. It is perhaps
unavoidable that men like Frank, of which there are too few,
cannot receive the nation-wide recognition and acclamation
that their accomplishments justly deserve. Be assured that
this recognition and acclamation rests in the hearts of all
of us here.

That he was an outstanding officer there is no doubt, but
he was also a true and loyal friend to me, and for this I am
extremely grateful. We have spent many hours together
exchanging views on everything from world government to skiing.
When Frank talked, his circle of friends usually listened,
because here was a man whose insight, imagination and logic
was undisputable; here was a man that the world needed to
help shape and improve it; and here was a man who mastered
a saying that I have always strived for "Mensch werden ist
eine Kunst".

I am now realizing too well that Frank is no longer
with us, but I am a better man because he was among us;
and so I pay my respects to him through you his family
whom he dearly loved, and ask each of you, Joyce, Michael,
David and Lindsay, to remember that while I am on this earth,
I am ready and willing to do all I can in making his passing
a little easier for you.

With sincere devotion and affection, I am, as ever,

Bill

rotated between a Norwegian and a Dane. If a Norwegian held the position, for instance, he would serve for three years, then, after his tour of duty was over, a Dane would replace him. General Bray's deputy was Lieutenant General Tufte-Jensen, a young, sharp Norwegian Air Force officer who arrived about the same time I did. Since the Norwegian and Danish armed forces were small and had relatively few senior grade officers, many of the officers were raised one grade when assigned to NATO. Tufte-Jensen was ordinarily a Major General who was temporarily promoted to Lieutenant General at NATO.

The Deputy Chief-of-Staff for Operations was a Danish Major General who was regularly a Brigadier General in the Danish Army. The Deputy Chief-of-Staff for the Air for AFNORTH was an American, Major General William Bell. I had the opportunity to write several speeches for General Bell during my tour and enjoyed working with him.

The highest-ranking German officer at NATO in Norway was Army Colonel Baron Christian von Tuempling, Deputy to the Director of Operations. I often worked closely with Colonel von Tuempling on briefings, and we became very good friends. Only Germans who had not been stationed in Norway during World War II could be sent to Norway as NATO officers. Colonel von Tuempling served in the German Army in Russia during World War II and related many of his experiences there to us. His perspective, having been on the Russian front before, was quite valuable.

My own deputy was a Frigaten Capitan, equivalent to Commander, Manfried Schlottveldt. He was a German and had been second in command on a submarine in World War II. He told me that he was always reluctant to sink ships in the North Atlantic because few men would survive. The waters were far too cold, and those left behind could die within 10 minutes. Manfried came from Northern Germany and told me that he once walked by a concentration camp there and asked the guard what it was. The guard's curt answer was, "Don't ask or you may end up in here yourself." He admitted that he never again tried to look into the concentration camp.

Manfried and I became good friends during our tour in Norway. Though his three daughters were older than Rachel and John, our families meshed well together and enjoyed the Norwegian countryside on many outings. We continued our friendship after we came back and corresponded regularly. Manfried later visited us in Dayton when he was there on an official visit. He retired a full Captain, equivalent to a full Colonel in the Air Force. He was a devoted naval officer, and his dream was to have his son follow in his footsteps. His son is now an officer in the German Navy.

I have always been ambivalent about German officers and their role in World War II because of the connection to the Nazi regime. In talking to them, I learned that many members of the military were apolitical. They were doing their job and had sworn to protect their country. I don't know what I would have done in their position. Regular German military officers, such as my friend Manfried or my World War I hero Count Felix von Luckner, were professionals who fought valiantly for their country and maintained their moral standards. The SS, which were the German Special Forces during World War II, were something entirely different. Loyal only to Hitler, the SS was responsible for the vast majority of heinous crimes committed. I tried to understand the German officers' position and did not try to judge them.

Twice during my stay in Norway, I was reminded of my disdain for the Nazis. Once, when I took my rent check to the owner of our house, he introduced me to a German manufacturer, a client with whom he was having drinks. I didn't like the man's looks. I knew he was in his early sixties and was old enough to have held a responsible position during the war.

"This German gentleman is a very important businessman," my landlord explained. "He employs thousands of people."

For the first time in my life, I could not bring myself to

shake hands with someone. Shortly before this meeting, I had seen a movie about slave laborers in Germany during the war. Intuitively, I felt that this businessman was just the type who would have used such laborers. I declined the invitation and left.

On another occasion, I picked up a poorly dressed hitch-hiker. As we drove, he volunteered that he had served in a German SS unit in Russia.

"Why would you volunteer for that duty?" I asked, surprised because the hitchhiker was not German. The Germans asked Norwegians and other conquered nationals to volunteer in their armies but didn't require service.

"I hated the communists more," the hitchhiker replied.

Taken aback, I stopped the car and asked the man to get out.

Many of our activities at NATO Norway fell under the heading of Top Secret. My area was most concerned with investigating new technologies. For example, after intelligence determined the Soviets were investigating a new series of missiles, it was my responsibility to find out what I could about the technology, its capabilities, likelihood of success, and possible usage by the Soviets. Security and communications also fell under my command. An entire section that reported to me was responsible for sweeping conference rooms for bugs, providing security passes and security investigations on NATO personnel, and conducting counterintelligence work in Norway. My final area of responsibility was intelligence planning—writing and maintaining the Intelligence Plan for AFNORTH, one of the most important documents that made up our War Plans at the time.

This plan hadn't been modified in five or six years and covered the entire AFNORTH—all of Northern Europe—and Colonel Engholm asked me to update it. To say the least, it was a challenge. I had never done anything like this before, but went to work on it doing the best I could. After reading the current plan, I found it to be excellent, well thought out, detailed, and comprehensive. Nonetheless, my superior thought it was too long. Finally, Colonel Engholm told me he wanted the revision finished before he left his command at the end of the year. It would take me the better part of my first year in Norway to work through the 600-page document.

The existing plan was quite detailed and some of the information did seem excessive—such as how to number prisoners of war, where to house them, and what to feed them. While I was able to reduce some volume, other material that dealt with estimates of the situation, most probable courses of action, and various alternatives if we went to war had to be updated.

For example, one of the major questions of AFNORTH was whether or not the Soviets would attack directly through Sweden and Finland or would go around the extreme northern part of Norway into Lapland and come down the Norwegian coastline. If the latter scenario were the case, would the Soviets use land forces, airborne forces, or amphibious forces, and at what points would they initially attack Norway? We had to make estimates or educated guesses of the Soviets' intentions. All of this information is still classified and can't be disclosed.

The Norwegian terrain was difficult to attack with many fiords and mountains and few usable ports or bases for the entire length of the Norwegian shore. Few bridges existed. More often, ferries transported people and vehicles across the fiords. In writing the plan, I had to consider all the options, possible courses of action for the Soviets, and provide alternatives to react to each possible course of action.

A considerable portion of my tour in Norway was spent in war exercises. We held a major war simulation approximately every three to four months, with the Soviets attacking in a different manner each time and AFNORTH reacting to the invasion. My role was often to write the intelligence scenarios for the exercises, deciding what kind of attack, from where, and with what forces. Sometimes I was part of the exercises and had the opportunity to respond to the scenarios.

I much preferred to actually be a part of the exercises. We received a variety of simulated signals from various Allied headquarters. From those signals and the given scenario, we created an Estimate of the Situation. Then we briefed the Commanding General on the scenario, the Estimate of the Situation, and our recommendations. During an exercise, the Intelligence, Operations, Signal, and other relevant officers briefed the General two to three times a day. He would query us and accept our recommendations or propose his own course of action.

AFNORTH was a pleasant assignment. Most of the command arrived around nine in the morning, left about four in the afternoon, and took a reasonable lunch break. While I was working on the War Plan, however, I was driven to complete the task. As I sat in the office into the early evening, all of my peers would pass by my office and say their goodbyes as they left for the day.

In addition to this challenge, I had other responsibilities. But eventually, I presented the rewritten plan, and my Colonel was pleased with the resulting material. The Norwegians also liked the plan and asked me to help them write their own Intelligence War Plan. Each of the governments represented subordinated themselves militarily to NATO, so the Norwegian plan was dependent upon the NATO plan I revised.

I visited Denmark to brief the Danish Defense Minister on the intelligence part of the War Plan. Unable to see me when I got there, the Defense Minister asked his Senior Intelligence Officer to debrief me. He was particularly interested in what this plan would cost Denmark to implement. After concluding that the additional cost was acceptable, he called the Defense Minister.

"I just talked to Colonel Cracken, and we can live with his plan," he said.

The Defense Minister replied, "Okay, in that case take him to lunch."

Over lunch, the Danish Intelligence Officer explained to

me that if the plan was going to be too expensive, I would not have been the guest of the government for lunch. The Danish were very frugal people.

Numerous times, I visited NATO Headquarters in Paris. One visit was on Bastille Day, July 14, while President de Gaulle was still in office. I was on my way to the airport and had the taxi driver drop me off near the parade route. I stood by to watch the French Foreign Legion and French Cavalry in all their finery march and ride down the streets of Paris. To me, the French National Anthem, "La Marseille," is the most stirring of all national anthems. I missed my plane that day, but I thoroughly enjoyed the festivities.

Colonel Engholm left a year into my tour of duty and Colonel Rollen from Norway took over as Assistant Chief-of-Staff for Intelligence. To the Danes and Norwegians, service in NATO was an important honor reserved for the finest officers. Colonel Rollen was one of Norway's greatest World War II heroes who had accepted the German surrender of Norway at the famed Arkahus Castle. This fort served as German headquarters during the occupation. It had previously been the home of the Norwegian Defense Ministry. Each September, during Norway's National Liberation Day, a national holiday, photographs of Colonel Rollen accepting the surrender are placed in all of the shop windows and printed in the newspapers.

AFNORTH headquarters was a multilevel facility built into a hill. The Officers' Club was at the top of the hill, and the main headquarters building was at the bottom. Colonel Rollen and I climbed that hill almost daily on our way to lunch at the club. I had four inches on the Colonel, but I always had a hard time keeping up with him. I taught Colonel Rollen a version of liar's dice played with coins. It was an interesting exercise to attempt to gain insights into the other players' strategies. At first, I let Colonel Rollen win, but too soon, he started beating me legitimately on a regular basis.

The Deputy Chief-of-Staff for Intelligence was a U.S. Naval officer, Captain Ben Johnson. He arrived in Oslo shortly after me, and we became good friends. Often we flew together in a C-47 up and down the Norwegian coastline, through the mountains and fog. However, Ben and Colonel Rollen didn't see eye to eye. Ben longed to return to flying and was not especially enamored with his NATO position. When Ben left, Colonel Rollen went to the Commander-in-Chief, General Sir Robert Bray, and requested that I be named as his Deputy. Since each position in NATO was designated by a country, a particular branch of the armed services, and a grade, that Deputy position was a United States Naval Captain slot. The Commander-in-Chief told Colonel Rollen about the hierarchy.

"Well, what can you do?" was Colonel Rollen's response.

The Commander-in-Chief wrote a letter to the U.S. Navy through our superior headquarters in Paris requesting that the Navy allow a U.S. Air Force Colonel to occupy the Navy slot. I had been promoted to full Colonel during my tour here. The Navy did not approve and was afraid of setting a precedent. The Commander-in-Chief wrote again, and eventually, the Navy accepted on the condition that when I left, the slot went back to the U.S. Navy. He readily agreed to the terms. This was one of the few times in the history of NATO that a slot was changed. I then became Deputy Assistant Chief-of-Staff for Intelligence for AFNORTH.

When I took over the slot, Colonel Rollen made me responsible for all conferences with Denmark, Norway, Germany, the United States, and England on any joint efforts.

U.S. Air Force Lieutenant Colonel Maygarden, an unassuming but brilliant officer, replaced me as Director of Plans and continued the job of maintaining the War Plans, coming up with some excellent ideas. I was so impressed that I recommended Colonel Maygarden for EWQ, Exceptionally Well Qualified, on his appraisal. General Bell, the senior U.S. Air Force officer at AFNORTH, and my direct American superior, was reluctant.

"We've got to be careful with these EWQs, Bill," he told me.

"But this officer is exceptional," I argued. "He is a fine officer."

Just before I left Norway, I discussed the situation with the General again.

"I agree with you," General Bell said, "he is sharp."

But to my recollection, Colonel Maygarden was never given an EWQ.

Upon my promotion to Deputy, one of my key assignments was to brief the Commander-in-Chief on intelligence matters. Fortunately, Sir Robert Bray had arrived in Norway about the same time I did, so both of us were learning the ropes at the same time.

Another part of my duty as Deputy was to be the Intelligence Briefing Officer for VIPs. This was a shared duty since AFNORTH had two briefing officers: one for Intelligence and one for Operations. Many VIPs, including on one occasion Vice President Lyndon Johnson, visited Norway during my tour. One of my most embarrassing moments was during Vice President Johnson's visit. He was in Norway to brief the parliament on the recent nuclear proliferation treaty with the USSR and came to our headquarters for a briefing on our operation. One of the areas I addressed was the geography of Norway, including the topography. I mentioned that the mountains there were about 13,000, but didn't indicate meters or feet. After the briefing, Vice President Johnson asked me which it was. I just froze. I hadn't thought about it. Quickly I said it was meters. General Tufte-Jensen corrected me politely, "Bill, we don't have mountains that high. It's feet." No one ever mentioned it again, but I am still embarrassed when I think about it.

Another time, the NATO War College visited us with officers from all 13 countries. Their escort officer told me to give my briefing slowly because some of the Turkish officers knew very little English. Apparently I overdid it. Toward the end of my presentation, I noticed my audience was getting restless, including the Commander-in-Chief. Afterward, he asked me politely but sternly why I was going so slowly. When

I told him it was for the benefit of the Turkish officers, he said it was still too slow.

Another responsibility I had was to supervise the Army, Navy, and Air Force Intelligence Divisions and their records and reports on the Soviet threat. The Soviets had their best mountain divisions located near the Norwegian border. The Norwegians had only a small standing army. When I flew north to examine the terrain, I often inspected army posts. These barracks were basically scattered huts containing at most a squad of men. Their purpose was not to fight the Soviets, but to perform a delaying action by dynamiting bridges and roads. This effort would buy time to allow Allied troops to arrive and establish a defense of Norway. When I inspected their barracks, I discovered that almost without exception, they all kept pictures of Prince Harold, who is now the King of Norway. Perhaps Prince Harold was so popular because he was a young man about the same age as many in the troops.

I remember on one trip to Lapland, I stood at the Soviet border and waved at the Soviet border troops just several hundred yards away. They waved back at me. They were just boys, so similar to the Norwegian troops they faced.

Once a year we conducted a major NATO exercise called Operation Viking Shield. The exercise simulated an actual invasion of Norway and the NATO response. In some instances, American Marines were flown in for the effort. This was, in effect, a full-scale dress rehearsal of World War III. The exercise was commanded from the Combat Operations Center and our special War Room called "the mountain." Midway up the hill where our headquarters was built was a dugout three-story facility large enough to maintain the entire NATO staff. Food and emergency supplies were stored there so we would be self-sufficient in case of war. The War Room was probably not sufficient to survive an atomic blast, but it was impervious to most any other bombs—even if struck with a direct hit.

Diplomats, politicians, and senior military officers from

every NATO nation attended Operation Viking Shield. The British and American Ambassadors to Norway were also typically there.

In a real situation, NATO alerts could be issued depending on the type of Soviet threat seen or upon various events that could occur. For every period of alert, certain activities would occur. For a certain alert stage, some forces would be deployed to Norway. For more severe alerts, greater and different types of troops would be deployed. All of this required constant planning and exercises. The Norwegians would permit foreign forces only under certain alert stages. If no alert existed or under lesser degrees of alerts, no troops—and particularly no nuclear weapons—could be brought into Norway.

The alert levels were DefCon 1, DefCon 2, DefCon 3, and so forth. DefCon stands for Defense Condition. The higher the number, the worse the condition. AFNORTH never received an alert past DefCon 3 while I was there. Several times, the Russians acted up. However, the DefCon level that would have caused troops or atomic weapons to be brought into Norway was never triggered. Troops were deployed into Norway only on a preplanned, periodic exercise basis and only after we alerted the Soviets that this was only an exercise. Even during the Cuban Missile Crisis in October 1962, AFNORTH never required deployment of troops into Norway.

When I was a Lieutenant Colonel, I rotated about once every six to eight weeks as after-duty hours Officer of the Day. When on duty, I slept on a cot in the mountain. If anything occurred during my duty, I first attempted to contact the Commander-in-Chief or his Deputy and other senior staff officers for orders. This plan gave AFNORTH a 24-hour, seven-day-a-week decision-making capability and reaction mode. Inside the mountain, we had a direct line to NATO Headquarters in Paris. Paris called us every hour on the hour to confirm the communications link. A full staff was present in the Operations Center at all times. The minute an alert was called, real or exercise, all military personnel involved rushed to the mountain. Once inside, the door closed and the people remained inside until the exercise or alert was completed. Families were left outside.

On the occasion of one of the Viking Shields, our British Major General, Chief-of-Staff of AFNORTH, asked a British Lieutenant Colonel and me to write his introductory presentation. The subject was the history of NATO and Soviet threats against us up to that time. He wanted us to go to Paris and dig up everything we could on crises since the beginning of NATO. We were busy dividing up the responsibility when a crisis erupted over Cyprus between the Greeks and Turks. The British were asked to mediate, and the Lieutenant Colonel was sent immediately to the crisis area to command a battalion. I was left to write the speech alone. I flew to Paris and researched the history of NATO and the alerts that had been called by NATO. After writing the speech, I made slides for visual aids. When the General delivered the speech, I operated the slides and felt a sense of *déjà vu* as I heard my own words, albeit spoken in an English accent. The speech was well received by all the VIPs at the conference, and I later received a commendation for the effort.

The British Defense Ministry allowed a number of NATO officers to attend their War College in Old Surrey, near Salisbury. General Bell selected me as one of those to attend. The three-week accelerated course was a simulated study of the deployment of British forces to intervene in a crisis in the Middle East. We made logistics studies of which and how many airplanes to use, as well as what troops to carry. During the day, the British were formal, but as the nights wore on, they were very relaxed, especially during a tradition called Dining In.

A Dining In was a party for officers working together. Women were not invited. While I was there, one of the Generals who attended was retiring and the Dining In became a roaring farewell party. The retiring cavalry officer stood on top of the table and made a speech. His fellow comrades all threw glasses at his feet. Once, during a Dining In, I engaged in an arm wrestling contest with a young Brigadier General. With all the eyes on the two of us, I felt it would be more diplomatic to allow the British officer to win.

As I looked him in the eye, I realized this was very important to him. All of his friends and fellow officers were watching. I had nothing to lose. These were not really friends to me. So I began to feel sorry for him and lightened my effort.

The only American witness was a Marine Lieutenant Colonel who was a fellow student at the school. He noticed when I quit and asked me, "What did you let him win for?"

"Well … " I began, hesitating.

"You could have beaten that limey."

"I thought he had a lot more at stake than I did," I said.

The British are big on tradition. While I was at the school, I had what the British call a batman, or officer's personal servant. When I got up in the morning, this Sergeant would have hot tea and bread waiting next to my bed and he would be pressing my uniform. When I got back to the barracks in the evening, he would be there with my pajamas ready. I tried to discourage the attention, but it was his job.

I was also selected by General Bell's office to attend NATO's advanced Special Weapons School in Oberammergau, West Germany for four weeks. Oberammergau is famous for its Passion Play, performed every 10 years. We didn't get to see the play, but did visit the theater and museum. Marilyn, the children, and our nanny, Dorothy, came along to Germany and stayed at a hotel in Garmish while I attended classes.

The final event at the school was a two-day finishing exercise, simulating a nuclear war. The students were given a plan and a certain number of forces to be deployed. We divided into a blue team and a red team. I was on the blue team, which was commanded by an American Brigadier General who selected me to be the Director of Operations and plan the entire deployment. The teams had limited resources, which we distributed between intelligence, combat units, and logistical support. When I presented our plan to the staff members of the school who acted as the umpires for the exercise, they complimented us. As a result, we thought we would win the exercise.

When the exercise was over, it ended in a tie, and we asked why we hadn't won.

"The Director of Operations for the red team did not do what you expected him to do," was the succinct answer.

The red team's Director of Operations was a highly creative and innovative game player. The game was set up so that the teams could not directly observe the deployments from the other side. In my role as Director of Operations, I had to determine where the opposition had deployed forces. I spent a large proportion of resources on intelligence prior to deploying and attacking, presuming that the forces would be where they would normally be in an actual invasion. The red team's Director of Operations did not oblige my assumptions. He put his entire forces, including air bases, on the border. This would never happen in reality. I did not attack those bases, but others further in the red team's operations area—bases I later found out were mostly empty. The red team knew we would not anticipate this move. It was well within the rules, but realistically it would have been a fatal strategy.

Our objective was to win a real war; their objective was to win the exercise.

I also commuted often to U.S. Air Force European Command in Wiesbaden, Germany, to maintain close liaison with U.S. Air Force Headquarters in Europe. Upon my promotion to Deputy, I was appointed as AFNORTH representative to the joint NATO Intelligence Board, which met in Germany to develop common intelligence procedures between the NATO nations. Generally the meeting was held in Munich. While I was there, I tried to talk myself into visiting one of the more infamous concentration camps outside of the city, but I couldn't do it. The idea of so many people suffering there kept me away. I still can't tolerate seeing people, especially children, suffer. I also hate to hear of animals being abused. I still turn off the television if anything like that is on. I just don't want to see it.

During our three years with NATO in Oslo, Marilyn and I had a very active social life. Everyone entertained all the time

Oslo, 1966. A typical dinner party.

and officers from each country appeared to be trying to outdo one another. The Danish officers received an allowance for housing and entertainment, and the Germans were given practically unlimited allowances. In Norway, the tax on Scotch was upwards of 500 percent, which meant it was priced well out of reach for the average Norwegian. However, NATO provided a whiskey ration to NATO personnel in Norway to be used for social occasions—four bottles of whiskey or scotch and eight bottles of wine per month. We got these from the NATO Officers' Club. As soon as I settled in and was told of the ration, I went in to buy my monthly allotment. At that time, I knew little about wine, so I asked the wine steward what he recommended.

"King Olaf was here two weeks ago. When he comes to the Officers' Club, we always have available a certain wine that he loves. I have six bottles left over. Would you like to have that?"

"Sure," I said, pleased to be lucky enough to get the King's favorite wine. I took the bottles home and opened up one with Marilyn. It was a red wine, and we thought it was much too dry. Still, the first party we had, we used up King Olaf's wine. I later had the opportunity to meet King Olaf when one of my Norwegian friends invited me to the Norwegian Officers' Club.

Marilyn and I were not heavy drinkers, and the ration was far more than we could drink ourselves. It even exceeded our party requirements. I often bought scotch and gave it to my Norwegian friends. I gave my landlord several bottles of whiskey as a thank you for using his car. I also met an Oslo police inspector at a ski lodge, and after becoming friends asked him if there was anything I could do for him.

"We just cannot afford whiskey because of the taxes," he explained.

"Come on over," I told him, "I'll take care of you." The inspector came over to the house, and I was happy to give him several bottles of scotch at the modest NATO price I had paid.

We attended at least two or three social functions each week, in addition to hosting our own dinner parties. By the time we left Norway, we had really had enough of the partying.

On several occasions, we were invited to General Bray's home for dinner parties. Typically, 12 high-ranking officers and prominent civilians and their wives would attend a party. At the last party we attended, shortly before we left, I was selected to sit to the left of Lady Bray, and Marilyn was seated to the left of General Bray. For a comparatively junior officer

The Commandant and Officers
of the
Joint Warfare Establishment, Old Sarum
request the pleasure of the company of

Lt Col and Mrs Cracker

at _the Defence College Akershus festning_
on _Tuesday 1st March_ at _7 p.m._ o'clock
cocktails R.S.V.P. P.M.C.

General Sir Robert and Lady Bray
request the pleasure of the company of

Colonel and Mrs L.W. Cracken

to _Dinner_
on _Monday 7th March 1966_
at _Villa Solborg Nesøya_

R.S.V.P. _EXT 421_
Aide-de-Camp to the Commander-in-Chief,
Allied Headquarters,
Kolsås, Oslo.

_7.45 P.M._
Black Tie.

NATO on the Russian Front, Norway, 1963-1966

With John on one of our ski trips.

to be asked to sit on the left side of the Commanding General was quite an honor. For Americans, to sit on the right side is an honor, for the British, the left is the honored side. Marilyn and I were amused to hear Lady Bray call her husband, "Bobby." General Bray was the picture of British aristocracy, very dignified with a full mustache. "Bobby" just didn't seem to fit.

Our closest American friends in Norway were Lieutenant Colonel Andrew Ritchey and his wife. Andy was a flying ace who received the Distinguished Service Cross for shooting down five German aircraft in one day. Despite his decorations and relative fame, he was a modest and laid-back fellow. His wife, Daphna, was a good friend of Marilyn's. They lived in Dallas upon retirement, and we visited regularly until Andy's death in 1996. He was a good friend and one of the men I admired most in the Air Force.

We skied extensively while in Norway, even John, who was just a small tike. He took to skiing as if he was born to do it. We did considerable cross-country and downhill skiing and participated in local contests. At one contest, everyone received an award for participation. Marilyn, whose skiing was modest, received a small cup. She was very surprised and appreciative to get an award.

"Why are you giving me an award?" she asked the dignified Norwegian judge who was the chairman of the event. "Is it because I fell so gracefully?"

"No, madam," he said. "You got the cup because you got up with such determination."

We also rented small boats to cruise along the coastline and fiords. Marilyn and I took many tours of Norway and Denmark and enjoyed the scenery and people very much. Marilyn also went to the Middle East with a group of other officers' wives while we were there.

We had several nannies while in Norway. Our last and favorite was Dorothy, from Holland. We tried to get Dorothy to come to the States with us when our tour was over, but she wouldn't, saying she would probably meet some American, fall in love, and marry, and would never get back to Europe.

Our neighbors in Norway were Ellen and Einnar Vegheim and their two children. The Vegheims were our best nonmilitary Norwegian friends. One Christmas Day, we looked outside in the snow and saw Santa Claus coming up our hill. It was Einnar coming to give our children gifts. Einnar and his family visited us in the United States. In 1993, he was stricken with cancer and died. We continue to be friends with Ellen and her new husband, Tor. They bought a winter home in Sun City near Phoenix, and we visit them or they visit us when they are in the United States.

I was very pleased to have the opportunity to get to know General Bray when I was in Norway. He was kind enough to send me a congratulatory note when I made full Colonel. Apparently he had heard some of my jokes at the Officers' Club, and he called me up one time and asked me for a favor.

"I'm going over to Danish Naval War College, and I need a

When I made full Colonel.

good joke," he said.

I provided two of my favorites to the Commander-in-Chief:

The Captain of the *Queen Mary* had captained the ship for over 30 years. His Executive Officer watched him all the time since he admired him and wanted to learn all he could before the Captain retired. Every morning, the Exec would watch the Captain open up the safe, take out an envelope, look at the message in it very closely, put it back in the envelope, and put the envelope back in the safe. Then the Captain would go to the bridge. The Exec was always curious about the letter. He figured it must contain instructions for the day.

From: General Sir Robert Bray, K.C.B., C.B.E., D.S.O., A.D.C.

Commander-in-Chief,
Allied Forces Northern Europe,
Kolsås,
Norway.

CINC/P/1   25 November, 1965

Dear Cracken

    I was most pleased to learn that you are to be
promoted to Colonel shortly. It is a promotion you
have richly deserved through hard work and loyal
service and I wish you every success in the future.

*Yours ever
Robert Bray.*

Lieutenant Colonel L.W. Cracken US AF
Intelligence Division

When the Captain finally retired and the Exec took over, one of the first things he did was go downstairs and open the safe. With a shaking hand, he took out the envelope and read the message:

It said, "Starboard is right. Port is left."

The General liked this joke especially because he was speaking to Navy officers. But I had another one for him:

NATO on the Russian Front, Norway, 1963-1966

The Captain of a U.S. Navy Destroyer was on maneuvers as part of a Carrier Task Force. He had a U.S. Senator on board. To impress the Senator, he wanted to show him how maneuverable his destroyer was. He wove his ship in and out of the carrier formations, zigzagging around the carriers. The Captain got a message from the Fleet Commander-in-Chief. A young Communications Officer brought the message up to the bridge.

"Captain, I have a message from the Commander-in-Chief," he said.

The Captain said, "Go ahead and read it."

But the Communications Officer insisted that it was a very personal message. "Wouldn't you rather be alone when you hear it?" he asked.

"We don't keep any secrets from the Senator, son. Read the message."

The message said, "Captain Smith, What the hell are you doing with your ship? Get it back into position or I will have you court-martialed."

The Captain, without changing expression, turned to the young Communications Officer, and said, "Son, decode that for me, will you?"

General Bray laughed and took both of them.

As my tour in Norway wound down, I was told that my next assignment would be in Washington D.C. at the Pentagon in a Senior Intelligence position. This position was a good step toward promotion to General. There was no guarantee, but the likelihood was good.

However, other events overtook those plans. In the fall of 1965, Marilyn's dad, who had diabetes and a serious heart condition, became gravely ill. He was not expected to live very long. Marilyn didn't know how sick he really was. In December 1965, her sister, Jony, called and told Marilyn to come immediately.

"Daddy's not going to live very long," Jony said.

Marilyn flew immediately to Dayton and stayed a month in New Carlisle before returning to Norway. When she got back, Marilyn asked me if we could forgo Washington and be transferred instead to Wright-Patterson Air Force Base to be close to her mother and dad. She left believing her father's illness would not be fatal.

I then requested a "compassionate" transfer to Wright-Patterson Air Force Base. In the military, these requests are available to accommodate personal problems. The only major caveat was that there must be a requirement for the person requesting transfer to the base. There was a position available at Wright-Patterson for my skill and grade. My earlier specialty was Aircraft Maintenance, and Wright-Patterson was the headquarters of the Air Force Logistics Command, which included in its responsibility supervising aircraft maintenance in the Air Force. The Chief-of-Staff of Intelligence was not particularly pleased, but approved the transfer.

Marilyn's dad died two weeks after she returned to Norway, on February 16, 1966. By this time, the transfer had already gone through and I didn't have the opportunity to change it. Four months later, we were in Ohio.

The Air Force and the Computer Age, Stateside, 1966-1973

Chapter Twelve

When we returned to the States and Ohio, I was too junior to qualify for one of the VIP brick homes on the base, so we bought a house on Zimmer Drive in Fairborn, a suburb just east of Wright-Patterson Air Force Base. It was a beautiful six-bedroom home in a friendly neighborhood. We quickly made many friends, the closest being the Dan Prices across the street. Dan was the navigator on the B-29 that is displayed in the Air Force Museum at Wright-Patterson Air Force Base.

My son, John, joined Webelos, a junior Cub Scout program, and we often went on overnight hikes with two young Captains at the base and their sons. John also played T-ball Little League. He was the catcher and first baseman. He was always a spirited member of the team. Rachel was a Girl Scout and involved in gymnastics, swimming at the base pool, ice skating during the winter at rinks at the base, and ballet.

Mary Van Morris, Marilyn's mother, lived only 15 minutes away from us. We saw her often. The children really enjoyed being close to their grandmother, having grown up overseas and far away in Maryland. My Aunt Em and Uncle John

Viscardi, who had both retired, sold their New York residence and moved to Dayton to be near us. This was a happy time for my family.

The Officers' Club at Wright-Patterson was one of the better ones in the country, and Marilyn and I socialized there often. Still, the level of social interaction was not close to what we had encountered in Norway. Despite my work schedule, I was able to attend every school open house and parent conference with Marilyn. In Fairborn, I was involved with the Big Brother program and was President of the Board of Directors of the Miami Valley Chapter of the Association for Children with Learning Disabilities.

At Wright-Patterson, I joined the Logistics Command. The Logistics Command is the largest command in the Air Force, employing hundreds of thousands of people. It provides support to all the Air Force commands both in the States and overseas. The command has six major Logistics Centers, including Wright-Patterson, Kelly in San Antonio, McClellan in Sacramento, Tinker in Oklahoma City, Warner-Robbins in Georgia, and Hill in Utah. Mobile teams also existed overseas to support overseas combat commands. The Logistics Command is responsible for all air depot work, major repairs for all units, as well as control of all supplies for the Air Force. When Israel went to war in the Middle East in 1967, for instance, it was our responsibility to provide it necessary equipment as directed by the President.

I reported to Colonel Lloyd Boatwright, who was Director of Computer Services for all of the Logistics Command. The Logistics Command probably had at that time one of the largest computer systems in the world. Computer Services had three major divisions encompassing primarily Supply, Transportation, and Aircraft Maintenance, each with a full Colonel in command. I was assigned as Director of the division responsible for Aircraft Maintenance. Also under my command were several other areas, including international sales and grants, a particularly pressure prone responsibility because we

The Air Force and the Computer Age, Stateside,1966-1973

had to meet all of the requirements Congress placed on us and couldn't go over the approved funding by even a dollar. The Logistics Command Controller, General Fred Morris, and my superior watched us like hawks. I had as my Deputy a GS-15, equivalent to Colonel, Carl Brooke, a 20-year veteran and expert logistician. Most of my staff of 800 was civilians. Together we were responsible for maintaining and redesigning all computers related to our area.

Carl Brooke helped me to learn the ropes, and we established an excellent rapport. His positive comments to Colonel Boatwright and General Morris helped to quickly establish me as an effective member of the group. When I arrived, I knew little about computers. I just knew what to ask and where to go to get the information I needed. Sadly, Carl Brooke died of a heart attack the first year I was at Wright-Patterson. Soon afterward, Colonel Boatwright called me in and said he had a replacement, a civilian from one of the other centers who was a genius in computers but was having some problems getting along with subordinates.

"Do you mind if I make him your Deputy?" he asked.

"No," I said, "if he is who you want."

Despite the man's problems at his former post, I liked him and did all I could to help him, even when his problems getting along continued under my command.

When I arrived, the Logistics Command was in the process of studying how to transfer its entire computer system from second generation to third generation computers. Second generation computers were tape driven, while third generation hardware used disks. This was going to be the first time we would have remote terminals on desktops. Prior to that time, data had to be entered and extracted directly from the main computer. This conversion meant our command was going to get the largest, most-modern computers made at the time. Only two vendors could provide the equipment needed: IBM and Control Data Corporation, CDC. This change spearheaded our efforts to completely revise the entire Logistics

Support System, making it less expensive and more responsive.

At this time, the massive logistics effort was traditionally "pull"-driven by a requisition system. One base might have one engine as a spare but really needed five or six; another base might have six or seven spares but only needed one or two. Some units were over-inventoried; others were under-inventoried. Aircraft were on the ground too long because of difficulties getting spare parts. Meanwhile, the badly needed spare parts were gathering dust in a warehouse at another air base. Our determination was to go to a "push" system, where parts were automatically sent to each unit based on previous experience, past records of usage, and current inventory. Push is a more complex, but more efficient system. Units only requisitioned for less costly, smaller items. The Logistics Command would estimate and anticipate need. Theoretically, this materially reduced inventory mismatches common to the pull system.

To accomplish this, the Command needed not only increased computer capacity, but also new software to make the entire system work. This was a revolutionary change for the Air Force and the largest undertaking of this kind in its history.

In 1967, General Fred Morris was responsible for creating a master plan for the Advanced Logistics System, as it was being called. This was no small task. Congress appropriated $500 million for the plan and its implementation, and it had to be approved by the Congress and the President. At this point, the plan called for a super grade civilian, equivalent to a General, or a General within the command to head up the planning effort for the conversion. Most of the senior people in the command shied away, not wanting to be associated with such a daunting challenge.

Before he died, Carl Brooke had told the General that I learned fast. Later, Colonel Boatwright, my immediate superior, recommended me to the General to head this master-planning effort. The General called me into his office and explained that this was a big plan and ultimately his responsibility.

"You've got planning experience, Bill," he said. "Prepare

me a rough idea of how the hell we can do it."

Then he tossed the planning guidelines documents to me. I prepared a short, optimistic, overly simplified outline for a plan and presented it to the General. Neither of us was particularly pleased, but it was a start. Nevertheless, soon afterward, General Morris called me at home and told me I was to head the master planning of this major conversion. He also assigned Clarence Dahm, a civilian and a logistics legend, to

---

3 October 1967

MEMORANDUM FOR RECORD

SUBJECT: Establishment of Work Groups Required by Activation of the Advanced Logistics Systems Center

1. Work groups have been established to define and coordinate actions concerning the Advanced Logistics Systems Center. The following assignments were made on 30 September 1967:

   a. Mr. Jack D. Brown, SGD; Mr. A. R. Bruckner, MCCP; Mr. John Ritner, MCCD, and other appropriate personnel will develop flow diagrams to depict the recommended flow of work through the Advanced Logistics Systems Center.

→ b. Colonel L. W. Cracken, SGDF, and Mr. Clarence Dahm, MCSY, will organize the resources and develop the methodology for preparation of the Advanced Logistics Systems Master Plan and will initiate work on the Master Plan.

   c. Mr. P. S. Dickey, MCOM, assisted by permanent representatives from MCGA, EWAC, SGOMW, and MCC will identify and act upon the placement and assignment of functions and individuals within the Advanced Logistics Systems Center, and other actions of a manpower, organization, and personnel nature.

2. The work groups will be manned as required by other directorates, staff offices, and 2750th AB Wg activities.

FREDERICK E. MORRIS, Jr.
Brigadier General, USAF
Commander
Advanced Logistics Systems Center

be my Deputy. Clarence had forgotten more about logistics than I would ever know. He was a critical asset to me.

After providing us with as many secretaries and clerks as we needed, the General then cut us loose, telling us we could take anyone else we needed from the Command to get the job done.

Clarence and I selected a large group of specialists from within headquarters itself, covering all areas of the Command's responsibility. General Morris also provided us with the services of three full Colonels, all who were senior to me. General Morris brought two of them in from outside the center. These officers were not overjoyed with the assignment. It would be a difficult, time-consuming project with a short deadline. It was risky at best. However, over time, and through working together on a daily basis, I won them over.

The project was not only a challenge because of its magnitude, but because we were on the cutting edge of technology, doing things with computers that had never been done before. The Air Force signed a contract with the RAND, a research group in California, to help with the more technical aspects of planning. We also worked closely with both IBM and CDC representatives.

After numerous planning meetings, our team decided to ask the General for even more people. We needed more experts in various fields and asked for the best talent from the other five Logistics Centers. We needed as many as 200 people across various skills. The General was shocked at our request.

"Do you realize what this is going to cost us?" he asked.

"Yes," I said, "but we need them to write the plan."

The General finally concurred and went before the Logistics Commander, his boss, a four-star General, General Jack Merrell. It was approved.

We identified 12 groups for systems analysis. They would determine the needs and specify what had to be done. Then programmers would convert these specifications into actual coding. In the end, nearly 800 people reported to me for creation of the master plan. Before we concluded, there was even a simulation of the proposed system to determine its feasibility and to note any possible problems or areas that could be improved. One Colonel was responsible for systems analysis and software design. Another Colonel was responsible for analyzing the demands and developing specifications for the hardware to allow bids to be sent out. The third Colonel was responsible for the simulations for the software. We met daily, together with Clarence, to discuss progress, problems, and needs.

During this time, I worked nearly 14 hours a day. Rachel referred to this as "the time the General took away my daddy." General Morris actually expected me to be available 24 hours a day. One night he came down to our offices at 2 a.m. and asked two of my Colonels where I was. I was actually at the office, but had stepped out for a restroom break. Knowing General Morris' temperament, I expected to be replaced during the project. I still find it a miracle that I lasted as Project Manager for the duration. General Morris was a tough customer, and my job was the toughest I faced in my career.

During these initial months, I rarely saw my family. The work was difficult and required long hours to solve the many problems that continuously occurred. Marilyn fixed the two children *middag*, Norwegian for early dinner, at 4 p.m. If I was lucky, I got to have dessert with the children just before they went to bed.

Our task force finally finished the plan on time and on budget. With many officials looking over my shoulder, I regularly had to brief generals and congressmen on the progress. Finally, I presented the master plan to General Merrell. The plan took almost six months of constant work and yielded five volumes: Volume 1, a general overview, summary, and history of the program; Volume 2, a detailed software package; Volume 3, hardware specifications; Volume 4, simulations; and Volume 5, an executive summary. The plan then went to Congress for the final stamp of approval. Those of us who worked so hard were all pleased when Congress approved the

Sunday
5 Nov 1967

Dear Bill,

This is just a quick note to thank you for all you've done for both myself and Jane. The year I spent working for you was the most enjoyable of the many years I've had in the AF. Now I'll make every effort to put your instructions to work for the AF in the future.

Bill, I really lucked into a job. You've probably heard that I didn't go to Phu Cat, instead I went to MACV. J-4 needed an OR type to guide 4 contract analysts in a study to develop Logistics Planning Factors in SVN. DOD plans to use the factors as guides for other bonish fires to plan for shipping and storage requirements.

The study will cover "through put" of all the ports. It will be really interesting because obtaining valid data by Commodity Class will be difficult. Statistics will have to be developed from samples.

The contract is being let to Planning Research Corp. In the last year their stock has risen from 13 to 60+. They have other contracts through the DOD Advanced Research Projects Agency.

Office hours are 7:30 to 19:30. (seven days a week) It takes 45 min each way by bus. I'm in a hotel in the Chinese section of Sagon. Ran into Jeff. Well so long for now. Give my best to all family

Sam.

plan. We had a lot of visibility, and it felt good to get the nod of approval.

The hardware specifications then went out for bids to IBM and CDC. CDC eventually won the award—one of the largest computer contracts ever awarded up until that time. The new computers required a complete change of infrastructure for the computer facilities since humidity, temperature controls, and auxiliary power units had to be installed for each of the six Logistics Centers.

Near the end of the process, I went worldwide to the Air Force Commands to brief their Commanders and staffs on the plan and how they would be effected. I had to sell each of them on the proposal since they would be involved. This strategy greatly aided in its final acceptance and implementation. Generally we were well received because we were going to save money and expedite getting equipment to those who

DEPARTMENT OF THE AIR FORCE
HEADQUARTERS AIR FORCE LOGISTICS COMMAND
WRIGHT-PATTERSON AIR FORCE BASE, OHIO 45433

REPLY TO
ATTN OF: MCG

SUBJECT: Letter of Commendation

17 April 1968

TO: ALSC (ACG/Brig Gen F. E. Morris, Jr.)

1. I would like to personally commend Colonel Louis W. Cracken, FR34920, of your command, for his outstanding contribution to the future logistics systems of the United States Air Force and to the Air Force Logistics Command's mission. On 1 October 1967, he was selected as Chief of the ALSC Logistics Systems Plans Office. In this assignment, he lead the development of the AFLC Advanced Logistics System Master Plan.

2. The development of this plan is one of the most important undertakings of its kind at AFLC in recent years and was the major initial task of the Advanced Logistics Systems Center upon its establishment on 1 October 1967.

3. The participants in this planning effort were carefully selected from the top logisticians and across many skills within the Command. Particular care was taken in selecting a small senior staff which would be responsible for the development, review, evaluation, and formalizing of the concepts, systems, and resource requirements; and for time-phasing the conversion. Colonel Cracken's exceptional leadership, creative imagination, and professional competence contributed significantly to the timely and successful completion of this momentous task.

4. This letter will be placed in his official personnel file.

JACK G. MERRELL
General, USAF
Commander

needed it.

I might add that before Congress approved the plan, we had to prepare a document showing the eventual savings in dollars to the Air Force budget. We estimated the expenditure of $500 million would result in approximate savings of $300 million every year in reduced personnel needs and inventory acquisition costs.

Reliability and Maintainability —
Achievement Through Program
Optimization

**1967-1968
General Conference
Management**

LESLIE W. BALL, *Chairman*
The Boeing Co.

FRANK A. THOMPSON, *Vice Chairman*
The Martin Co.

R. E. LEDBETTER, *Program Chairman*
General Electric Co.

STANLEY A. ROSENTHAL, *Chairman*
Publications Liaison
Kollsman Instrument Corp.

CHARLES W. RUSSELL, *Chairman*
Past Chairman's Advisory Committee
Aerospace Corp.

HARRY R. KATTELMANN, *Chairman*
ASME San Francisco Section

CARL HANDEN, *Chairman*
ASME Santa Clara Section

**1967-1968
Steering Committee**

JOHN E. LOSEE, *Chairman*
Douglas Aircraft Co.

R. E. LANIER
LTV Aeronautics

CMDR. DONALD M. LAYTON
Naval Postgraduate School

LIONEL LEVY
Aerospace Corp.

F. E. MARCH
The Boeing Co.

C. W. RUSSELL
Aerospace Corp.

R. E. SHARP
Ryan Aeronautical Co.

LESLIE W. BALL
FRANK A. THOMPSON
Ex-Officio Members

**SEVENTH
RELIABILITY AND MAINTAINABILITY
CONFERENCE**

July 14-17, 1968 • Jack Tar Hotel • San Francisco, Calif. 94101

August 1, 1968
Please reply to:

Leslie W. Ball
Director of Product Assur
The Boeing Company
Aerospace Group
P.O. Box 3999
Seattle, Washington 98124

General J. G. Merrell (MCG)
Commander Air Force Logistics Command
Wright Patterson Air Force Base, Ohio 45433

Dear General Merrell:

Please accept my sincere appreciation for the outstanding contribution to the success of the 1968 Reliability and Maintainability Conference provided by the representatives of the Air Force Logistics Command.

As you know the agreement for AFLC to make a panel presentation under the title "Response to Military Operational Experience" was developed by General Gerrity and the Conference Management Committee which it was my privilege to chairman. I am sure that Tom would have been proud of the content and effectiveness of the presentations by General McCoy and Colonels Weeks, Chapman and Cracken.

One of the major objectives of the plenary session of this Conference is to increase the dedication of the attending engineers to the work that they are doing, particularly for the Department of National Defense. John McCoy's AFLC team fully achieved this objective.

Yours respectfully,

Leslie W. Ball.

Leslie W. Ball

SPONSORED BY: SOCIETY OF AUTOMOTIVE ENGINEERS, INC., AMERICAN SOCIETY OF MECHANICAL ENGINEERS,
AND AMERICAN INSTITUTE OF AERONAUTICS AND ASTRONAUTICS, with the participation of

The Air Force and the Computer Age, Stateside,1966-1973

Once the plan was approved, its implementation was a whole new battle. Sixty people worked for me in the planning office. Together we were responsible for amending the plan as needed to ensure its implementation. As new ideas and suggestions arrived, we accepted or denied them. If the suggestions were accepted, we incorporated the ideas into the plan. After the plan was completed, I became Director of Plans. My new Deputy was Dwight Arnold, one of the top five logisticians in the Air Force.

During this time before we began to implement the plan, I was assigned as a special aide to our Commanding General at the joint Army-Navy-Air Force Logistics Planning Conference in Washington, D.C. The aides' panel included an Army Colonel and a Navy Captain. The Navy Captain, a former aircraft carrier commander, served as our chairman. The Marines also occasionally sent a representative. This group decided the agenda and the items to be discussed at the Joint Logistics Command meetings of the three services' Logistics Command Commanders. As aides, we would sit behind our Generals providing information as needed. The Generals then discussed joint logistics matters.

This was a prestigious job since this group made plans for all joint military logistics. We discussed problems and created guidelines. The aides played an important advisory role since these Generals did not have the time or the information to make the decisions on their own. Once, I was listening to the four-stars discuss logistics matters and decided to make a pertinent comment to the Army General. The General was not warm to the interruption, and I decided afterward to keep quiet at future meetings.

During my tour, General Morris could not attend one of the annual meetings of the Air Force Worldwide Material Conference at Vanderburg Air Force Base in California, which included all Commands in the Air Force, both stateside and overseas. This was during the time when the military faced bad publicity about $600 toilets and $300 hammers. This conference addressed many issues common to all Air Force Commands in the area of logistics support. One area of discussion was to reduce the number of equipment orders requiring expensive specifications. If a company had to retool to make a certain nut and bolt for the Air Force, the initial cost was immense. It was better to buy off-the-shelf items if possible. At this annual conference, all the chiefs of the major Logistics Commands met to share other ideas as well. General Morris was the usual Logistics Command representative, but on this one occasion, he sent me in his place. All of the commanders were Generals. With General Morris' speech in hand, I was the only Colonel to make a presentation. I started out my presentation with a joke that was not part of the prepared speech:

"I know you gentlemen are sorry to see Fred Morris is not here, but at least you won't lose your money to him this year." The Commanders would traditionally play a round of golf while at the conference. I didn't realize until later that this joke got a big laugh because General Morris was not always that lucky. I was a little sensitive about just reading someone else's speech, but apparently it didn't appear that way. At dinner later that evening, one of the aides told me he thought mine was the best extemporaneous speech made. It was just another meeting to the Generals, but to me it was a highlight. I did play golf with some of the aides and typically lost.

Team-building was a big part of keeping my group going through this difficult and often frustrating implementation process. When I had gone through the War College in England, I was impressed by the team-building tradition they called Dining In. I suggested we put on such a social event for the officers. These informal gatherings didn't include spouses. I suggested a Dining In to General Morris, and he agreed it was a good idea.

I was too busy, so another Colonel was assigned the job. But since he had never been to a Dining In, he asked me to help him plan it. I told him we had to have a physical challenge at some point in the night and suggested Indian wrestling. During the Dining In, I demonstrated the main event of the evening to all of the attendees. I asked the officers to make two lines facing each other, and to wrestle the man directly across from each of them. After each pair finished, the winners would again line up against each other. Eventually, out of the 60 or so officers, only four were left. Since I had considerable experience at this challenge, I was one of the four. In the semifinals, my opponent was a tall, thin, young Captain. He had been watching me and employed an unusual strategy. He let me lower him to a certain point, then when I had almost pinned him he used his considerably longer arms to get me off balance. As I pushed and pushed him with my shorter arms, my foot slipped over the line and I was disqualified. He outsmarted me and won fair and square. By this time, though, I had become self-conscious. I really didn't think I should win since I'd suggested the event. My worthy opponent went on to win the entire event.

By the beginning of 1969, the start of my fourth year at Wright-Patterson, the logistics plan was in good shape. One of my friends at the time was the Associate Director of the Air Force Institute of Technology at Wright-Patterson, equivalent to a Vice President of a university. He was retiring and told me he would put in a good word for me with the Commander, a two-star General. I had always admired the Institute and had occasionally guest-lectured there. To my delight, the Air Force approved me for the position.

I approached General Morris and asked him to approve the transfer.

"You're never going to make General over there," Morris retorted.

"Stay here," was General Morris' final word, implying he had future plans of his own for me. He was extremely interested in following up on the computer conversion plan and getting it implemented. We had talked about it for an hour or so, and the General eventually talked me out of the transfer.

I had other reasons for staying with General Morris. He

was an extremely tough manager and unpopular with many of his subordinate officers. He had 10 Colonels working for him. Every single Colonel that had been there when I arrived was no longer working for him. They had either retired or transferred. I said to myself, "If I desert the General now, the other Generals might say he can't keep a Colonel working for him. But if I stay, he'll at least be able to say he had me." I didn't want to do that to him. He was a very dedicated and tough officer, and I personally liked him.

General Morris had practically adopted Marilyn, and the two of them had a running joke about both of them being from the Morris clan. He had a sister, Vy, who had died, and he often said Marilyn reminded him of her. Marilyn and Mary Van (her mother) used to escort the General's mother whenever she came to visit him in Dayton. General Morris gave me the opportunity for promotion by frequently inviting me to socialize with the other Generals. Networking and relationships are important elements for Colonels to make General.

While at Wright-Patterson Air Force Base, I received my formal promotion to permanent Colonel in the Regular Air Force. Up to this time, I was officially a temporary Colonel and a permanent Lieutenant Colonel. This was a system that really did not affect my pay or retirement grade. It was important only for promotion purposes. Brigadier General promotions were generally limited to permanent Colonels. About one-third of temporary Colonels in the Regular Air Force were promoted to the permanent grade, which required the Senate's approval by individual name. The temporary promotions did not.

My friend at the Institute left and went to Wright State University in Dayton, where he became the Vice President for Planning. Later, when I was contemplating my options, I considered retiring in Dayton and teaching at Wright State, a new university. I talked to the President of the university and he said he would consider giving me a position when my plans were more firm. I never followed up.

At Wright-Patterson, I also ran into Dean Hess, my old

DEPARTMENT OF THE AIR FORCE

AIR FORCE INSTITUTE OF TECHNOLOGY (AU)

WRIGHT-PATTERSON AIR FORCE BASE, OHIO 45433

REPLY TO
ATTN OF: AFITSL-C

17 MAR 1970

SUBJECT: Letter of Appreciation

TO: AFLC (MCC)

1. I wish to express my appreciation to Colonel L.W. Cracken of your Research Division (MCCTR) for his presentation to class members of Course 358, "Computer Simulation for Logistics Managers." Colonel Cracken's efforts were well received by the students and our course director has informed me that his presentation motivated the students to make this one of the best received offerings of this course.

2. This is the first opportunity Colonel Cracken has had to participate in Course 358. We appreciate his keen interest and enthusiasm and look forward to his participation in future offerings. Your support of the School of Systems and Logistics is greatly appreciated.

FOR THE COMMANDANT

JOHN J. APPLE, Colonel, USAF
Chief, Continuing Education Division
School of Systems and Logistics

Strength Through Knowledge

friend from the recruiting days in Kentucky. Dean was the Public Relations Officer and a senior full Colonel for the Logistics Command. He was in the process of retiring to teach school in a nearby school district in Ohio. Dean wanted me to replace him in the public relations office, but ultimately our Commanding General did not approve.

Juggling these various options, I didn't have to contemplate the future long before family matters suddenly made it clear. In 1968, Marilyn began to suffer severe symptoms of multiple sclerosis. She could hardly walk. She had noticed the first symptoms of MS even before we married. When she was 24, her foot went to sleep and stayed that way for several weeks. When she was in graduate school, her whole right arm and hand went numb. She couldn't write or hold onto anything. Doctors didn't know what it was. They decided it was just anxiety because she was a graduate student. The numbness did finally go away. Then after we married, in England her right arm went to sleep again. The numbness and soreness lasted for two weeks, then, suddenly, everything went back to normal.

Marilyn saw an Air Force neurologist at that time. He suggested she see a British psychotherapist. I had been moonlighting teaching Industrial Management for the University of Maryland campus in England at night, and that's where the extra money went. Marilyn saw the psychotherapist for three or four months until we left for Maryland. While we were in Norway, Marilyn was always tired. Later, we found out that is typical of multiple sclerosis—a giveaway symptom.

During our stay at Wright-Patterson, Marilyn began to have trouble walking. Frequently she drove Rachel to the grocery store, gave her a list and a blank signed check, and waited for her while she did the shopping. No doctor we consulted helped. Frustrated, Marilyn said she wanted to see a neurologist again. Not long after she walked in the door, the neurologist told Marilyn she had multiple sclerosis. He confirmed his diagnosis with a number of tests. While MS gets worse with age, the cold climate in Ohio was also aggravating the condition. Marilyn was in the hospital several times during the latter stages of our stay in Dayton.

In researching MS, I discovered that the best place for MS patients is in a warmer climate. I inquired immediately of bases in the South. One of the Logistics Centers was Kelly Air Force Base in San Antonio, Texas. Near Kelly was the Air Force's Wilford Hall Medical Center, one of the best military hospitals in the nation. San Antonio also provided a warm climate.

In 1969, after Marilyn's condition became known, I went to General DeLuca, since General Morris had been transferred to Washington by this time, and explained the situation. I respected him and we had quickly become good friends. Marilyn and Mrs. DeLuca also got along well. Both were interested in the Association for Research and Enlightenment, Edgar Cayce's organization.

"I'd like to go to Kelly," I told him.

"But we don't have much chance for promotion there. The Commander and the Deputy are both Generals and they're not going anywhere for a while. The only other possible General slot is actually a Colonel's slot that leads to General. It's Director of Materials Management, the number three job. I'll recommend you if you want it."

I knew the job since Kelly was one of the Logistics Centers I had visited in briefing the field officers on the ALS plan. I even knew the current officer there who was about to leave. It was one of the toughest jobs in the command. He controlled all of the activities at the base. It was a 70-hour a week job.

But I had made up my mind. I needed to take Marilyn to a warmer climate and a top-notch medical center. She was my first priority.

"Now, look," the General told me in a fatherly tone. "There's the Air Force and there's your family. You've got to decide which one comes first."

"I'm really not going down there to get promoted, sir," I replied. "Where do you think I'm needed most?"

"If you do go down there, the best position for you is Director of Computer Services. If you take it, then we will make Kelly the pilot site for the Advanced Logistics System."

"I think that would be better, sir, than the Director of Materials Management in light of my wife's health," I said thanking him.

The officer that ended up taking the Materials Management job was another officer from Wright-Patterson who was junior to me. Eventually he made Brigadier General and returned to Wright-Patterson where he made Major General as Chief-of-Staff. Later he moved to the Pentagon as Director of the Defense Logistics Agency in Washington and became a Lieutenant General. I sometimes thought this could have been my path, but I never regretted my decision to take a less demanding post so I could be more of a help to Marilyn.

With Kelly now the test site for the first installation of the new computers, I was reassigned there as Director of Computer Services.

We moved to Quiver Drive in San Antonio, Texas, in August 1970. As one of the senior Colonels at the base, I was not only entitled to base housing at Kelly but was actually expected to live on the base. I was originally assigned a house between the two Generals, the Commander and the Vice-Commander of the Logistics Center. Although it was a beautiful home, it did not have central air conditioning, but rather window units and ceiling fans. They would not have been helpful to Marilyn's condition. I also wanted a pool for Marilyn to do her exercises. I asked the Commanding General for a waiver due to Marilyn's condition. The General approved the waiver but required me to live no more than five miles or 15 minutes traveling distance from the base. If there was a computer problem at the base, I had to be available on a 24-hour basis.

The home on Quiver fit all of our requirements. It was all on one level, was near enough to the base, and had room in the backyard to build a swimming pool. We have been planning to move all these years, but we are still there.

My Aunt Em and Uncle John stayed in Dayton only a few months after we moved to San Antonio. Then they moved to San Antonio and purchased a condominium in the city. Our relationship continued to get closer as we spent more and more time together. When Uncle John retired, his lifetime collection of books amounted to several thousand volumes. He did not want to take the books to Dayton when he retired. He offered them to me, but I didn't feel that I should own such an important reference library. It deserved greater public access. Nor did I have room in my home for the large collection. Uncle John offered the collection to Columbia University, his alma mater. They accepted his offer but would not agree to his stipulation to keep all of the books together. Uncle John offered the collection to several other U.S. universities, but none could accommodate it as a whole. Finally, while on their semiannual visit to Nice, France, they visited Malta Island. While there he contacted the University of Malta. A poor school, they were

Bronze relief, University of Malta John E. Viscardi Engineering Library.

delighted to have his books and readily agreed to his terms. The University of Malta set up a John Viscardi Wing in the Engineering Library and housed his collection there. Uncle John obtained the services of an Italian artist to make a bronze relief of him and Aunt Em to be placed at the entrance to his room in the library.

Until they moved to Ohio, Aunt Em and Uncle John had lived six months in New York and six months in Nice where they rented an apartment on the Rue de les Anglais, a main thoroughfare. They were going to buy the apartment and badly wanted us to move to Nice with them. They even offered to pay all of our expenses and buy two apartments, one for them and one for us. At the time, though, our children were still small, and I would have had to retire from the military and become somewhat dependent upon my aunt and uncle. I respectfully declined the offer. Aunt Em and Uncle John gave up the apartment in Nice and moved initially to Dayton and then to San Antonio. Later, in San Antonio in 1976, Uncle John had a stroke and was committed to a nursing home. Aunt Em took the bus every day to the nursing home to visit and take care of him. Uncle John died in October 1980, and Aunt Em followed a few months later in February 1981. At both their funerals, I gave the eulogy.

Unlike the Viscardis, Marilyn's mother never considered moving to San Antonio. She had a nice home, and all of her friends were in New Carlisle. However, in 1982, Mary Van's age began to show. She decided to sell her house, give up housekeeping, and move to live with her youngest daughter Jony. It was highly likely that if Marilyn had not had MS, Mary Van would have moved in with us. By 1990, Mary Van's condition had worsened, and she entered a nursing home. She died on Christmas Day in 1992 and was buried in New Carlisle, next to Marilyn's dad.

Upon our arrival at Kelly, Marilyn was still not doing well and entered the hospital. She stayed at the Air Force's Wilford Hall Medical Center for a week. Wilford Hall did not special-ize in MS, nor does any other military hospital. However, it did have an outstanding neurological department. The doctors said there was not much they could do for Marilyn and sent her home. At home, she began hallucinating. While she was at Wilford Hall, the doctors had given her a heavy dose of steroids. To correct the situation, the military doctors sent her to a special civilian hospital. She was there for several weeks. Once the medication level was in balance, she returned home.

During my time at Kelly, Marilyn was in and out of the hospital several times. The doctors tested various drugs and therapies on her. Some worked for a short time; some didn't work at all. I wanted to be there to observe her, to know firsthand which were favorable and which were causing adverse reactions. They were not treating the disease as much as the symptoms, and it was frustrating to both of us.

When I went down to San Antonio for a visit after I knew I would be assigned there, I asked my friends there if they knew of a capable housekeeper we could hire to help Marilyn. One recommended Josie Lopez, who worked for another military officer who had just been transferred, and was now available. She had a long waiting list of clients. I interviewed her and we just clicked. I told Josie of Marilyn's problems, and she was sympathetic. She said, "I can work for you two days a week. That's all I can do." We hired her. Twenty-eight years later, she still works for us two days a week. She is family. She has high regard for us, and we love her. Once, at a country club, we were introduced to another couple, Mr. and Mrs. Wheately. He is a prominent local attorney. They looked at us wide-eyed and said, "You're not THE Crackens are you?"

"We're Bill and Marilyn Cracken," I replied.

"Does Josie Lopez work for you?"

"Yes, she does."

"She works for us, too, and she talks about you frequently. We're happy to finally meet you."

Rachel and John looked upon Josie as a second mother, especially during those years when I was working hard and

Marilyn was ailing. They often turned to Josie for advice.

Despite my plans to spend more time at home, my job often kept me at the base late into the evening. The San Antonio Logistics Center was responsible for logistics support of the entire Air Force and had a worldwide responsibility. As Director of Computer Services I was responsible for all of the computers on the base supporting the Air Force worldwide, as well as those on the flight line and all computers involved in testing equipment for engines and aircraft maintenance. As the pilot site for testing the ALS, I also began to implement the plan I had helped write, and supervise the installation of the new large-scale CDC mainframe computers. The computers were housed in a beautiful new building that was humidity- and temperature-controlled and had its own power backup system. It was, at that time, one of the most advanced systems not only in the Air Force, but also possibly in the entire world. In addition to daily supervision of the construction of the building and installation of the computers, I briefed both the Commanding General at Kelly and the Logistics Command back in Dayton on the pilot program's progress.

In the meantime, I still had the responsibility of maintaining the existing computers and software, not only within the Center at Kelly but our entire area of responsibility. When I arrived, most of the computers were old and still used tapes. A considerable part of our work force was key-punch operators. We also had numerous analog computers being used to test engines and various aircraft structural problems. This was a critical area. If the computers shut down, it not only effected the entire base of over 20,000 people, but hampered our ability to provide logistics support for the Air Force worldwide. It was not unusual to get a call in the middle of the night from the Commanding General at Wright-Patterson if even one of the computers went down temporarily.

Unscheduled downtime was a nightmare I tried to avoid at all costs. When it did occur, I was on 24-hour duty until the computers were back up again. And to think this is where I thought I would relax and enjoy my family!

My third major area of responsibility was the software development for the Aircraft Maintenance Area for the ALS, which had not been totally completed. While I was still at Wright-Patterson, I had delegated some of the software development to the Air Force Logistics Center at San Antonio. It was the Center responsible for the Aircraft Maintenance software system. We created a separate branch that worked on this area of software. It was located in East Kelly, some distance from our computer complex.

I also sat on the Engineering Board. Whenever new programs arrived at Wright-Patterson, the board decided whether Kelly or another depot would develop the program. For example, when an engine-testing procedure was devised for a new engine coming into the Air Force inventory, the board decided which of the Centers would be responsible for its maintenance.

When I first arrived at Kelly, I told my civilian Deputy that I wanted all of the people who worked for me to assemble in the auditorium so I could greet them.

"Do you know what that will cost the government to pull them off the job?" he asked.

"I don't care. I want it," I said.

Though I didn't consider this an extraordinary practice, this was the first time it had ever been done at Kelly. I introduced myself and gave the group a short pep talk. I didn't say anything fancy, just provided a personal touch. I thought this was an important gesture to indicate that I view people as individuals, not as numbers.

Not long after I arrived, General Jack replace General Ridell as the Commanding General at Kelly. He was reassigned from Logistics Command Headquarters. His immediate priority was to improve inventory control at Kelly. I was assigned to head a study in this area. I was already busy on the pilot project for the ALS and had to maintain the computer systems. I told the General I was already working more than full time, hoping to dodge the new project. Nevertheless, he assigned me to the task. It was *déjà vu* all over again. The General assigned me five of the top civilian logisticians on the base for the project.

I found out later that General Jack had a hidden agenda. He was considering me to ultimately become Director of Engineering. It was an upward move.

I proceeded with the study along with the logisticians assigned to me. In some areas, I was not pleased with their performance and had to constantly cajole and try to motivate them to do better. Sometimes I had to ask them sternly and repeatedly to revise parts of the report I thought were inadequate. Only under this intense pressure were we able to complete the project on time, on budget, and to my satisfaction.

The report was well received by the General, but I didn't get the new post. Our headquarters, without consulting our General, had assigned an incoming Colonel. This Colonel was senior to me and was an Aircraft Maintenance veteran. I was not heartbroken at the time since I was too busy trying to complete the pilot project under some tight deadlines. Assignment as Director of Engineering instead of remaining Director of Computer Services would not have resulted in a promotion, but would have been more prestigious.

I was also involved in a number of civic duties while I was at Kelly. In 1972, two senior civilian logisticians and I were asked to select Miss Kelly Air Force Base. I was made chairman, but I was uncertain how to go about the process. The other two gentlemen had done this before and suggested to me that it would be nice if Miss Kelly and her two attendants represented a rainbow coalition—one African American, one Hispanic, and one Caucasian. I agreed, and we ended up with an African American Miss Kelly, and an Anglo and a Hispanic attendant.

Being politically correct was not always *de rigueur*. When I first arrived, I had numerous senior civilian professionals working for me. One who happened to be Hispanic was in line to be promoted. Three of my civilian Branch Chiefs came to me and told me this man was being promoted primarily because he was Hispanic. They said they didn't think he was right for the position.

The position reported to me. I had just arrived and did not know all the facts.

"The Hispanics were here long before we were here," I told them. "They are entitled to the senior positions, too."

Their response was that three-quarters of the Hispanic population in the area were only first or second generation Americans.

"Sure," they continued, "there were Hispanics here before the Anglos came, but this area of Texas was a sparsely populated area. This massive Hispanic population in San Antonio is comparatively new. Many of them came after the Anglos developed the area," they argued.

I called them off. "I'm not going to get into the middle of this. Just forget it." I gave the man his promotion.

Once, an alcoholic Hispanic worker went AWOL (Absent Without Leave). After he failed to report to work, the situation was brought to my attention. However, since we couldn't find him, we couldn't fire him.

I was exasperated. This seemed ridiculous to me.

"We've got to give him a letter saying he's been fired," I was informed.

Finally, the man was found and brought before me. His supervisor had already advised me to give him a break because he had a family and had promised he would not drink anymore.

I was certainly willing to give the man another chance. If I had fired him, I expect it would have ignited some intense feelings of racial discrimination as well as an investigation and days of paperwork and depositions. It was just not worth the potential ramifications, especially given the possibility of ruining this man's life. So, I gave him another chance and never regretted it.

One of the most difficult situations I encountered at Kelly

was when one of my workers committed suicide. Afterward, I wrote a letter to each of my workers, all 800 of them, and told them, "Your workplace should be like your family. We sometimes spend more time together at the workplace than we do at our own homes with our own families. Let's stick together. If anyone hears of anyone having problems, please let me or your supervisor know about the situation."

I signed each letter personally because I wanted them to know how much I cared. I wanted to do everything possible to avoid another tragedy. Every one of the people who worked for me was important to me, and I felt an obligation to do my best to take care of each of them.

I told my administrative assistant that I wanted the letter to go out to every single worker, individually addressed.

"That will cost a lot of money, Colonel," he warned.

It was worth every penny.

When my Deputy retired after 30 years of service, the headquarters took action to replace him. The job required a rank of GS-15. Several people recommended a GS-14 at our Sacramento Logistics Center, a woman named Beverly Jacobsen. I sat on the Promotions Board and agreed it would be a good time to have a woman GS-15. She was hired and promoted, becoming the first woman GS-15 in the Logistics Command. She made an outstanding Deputy.

My personal administrative assistant was Mr. C.E. Stubbs, called Stubby. He is now President of the Texas Homeowners Association. We became very good friends. Being a fanatic fisherman, Stubby used to take my son, John, and me fishing at Buchanan Lake.

As 1973 approached, I was "over the line" by military standards. Timeliness is everything in the Armed Forces. When you reach a certain grade and still have not been promoted, you lose momentum. The usual retirement grade for career officers was Major or Lieutenant Colonel. If you don't make Major by the 21st year, you are out. If you don't make Lieutenant Colonel by the 23rd year, you're out. You can't make it to

The Air Force and the Computer Age, Stateside,1966-1973

30 years unless you are a full Colonel. For the first time in my career, some of my peers as Colonel were junior to me but were also senior to me in responsibility. I was not used to such a situation, and I didn't like it.

In 1973, the pilot program was not doing as well as it should have been because the deadlines were too optimistic. A new General who was not knowledgeable about the ALS replaced the old ALS Center Commander, General DeLuca, who had replaced General Morris. Due to the new General's inexperience, he was not able to provide the type of support necessary for timely implementation of the ALS.

I went to the semiannual ALS meeting at Wright-Patterson to meet the new Commander as well as all of the other senior officers involved in ALS development worldwide. Of all the participants in that meeting, I was the only one who had been with the project since its inception. In the first meeting with the new General, someone asked what "ALSX" meant. I was the only one there who knew the answer. The system itself was called ALS. While we were developing the plan, we didn't know whether IBM or CDC would be manufacturing our computers, so we just called the computers ALSX.

The General was pleased to finally know what that meant.

Since I was the officer in charge of the pilot program at Kelly, and at one time was responsible for the master plan, this meeting was somewhat deflating to me. While having lunch on the last day of the meeting, I sat next to the General and tried to fill him in on some of the major problems. Since he didn't ask my advice, he didn't take it as well as I would have liked. His main concern was to meet the timetables assigned him. I have always felt that the Air Force should have retained General Morris until the project was complete. Bringing in two new commanders during the implementation process was part of the reason we were having difficulty meeting the deadlines.

Having a good rapport with General Ridell, the Commanding General back at Kelly, I did everything I could to meet the deadlines, even though I knew they were overly optimistic.

Once when General Ridell and I were both at Wright-Patterson for a meeting, we had drinks with some other officers at the Officers' Club. This was about the time when Lieutenant Calley had just been court-martialed for the infamous My Lai massacre of the Vietnam War. Everyone at the table, including the General, thought that the Court-Martial Board was wrong to convict him for commanding the force that opened fire on the villagers, including women and children. The consensus was that in war, your first goal was to protect your troops and sometimes, lacking all information necessary to make the right decision, anything goes.

"How could Calley know whether some of those older men, women, or children in the hamlet carried guns or hand grenades? How did he know they wouldn't shoot at them?"

Perhaps I should have kept quiet. But using poor judgment, I voiced my opposing view. I couldn't ignore the horror of My Lai.

"General," I said, "in my experience, I have never seen old men, women, or children throw hand grenades or shoot at troops. I think perhaps Calley overreacted due to lack of experience and pressure."

I don't think my argument changed anyone's mind, including the General's. It was the wrong thing to say at the wrong time.

For several weeks, our relationship changed. Before at staff meetings, the General asked for and considered my input. Afterward, I began to feel distanced.

Several weeks later, I mentioned to the General that I felt the timetable for the development of the aircraft maintenance software was too optimistic. I told him it was possible we would miss the deadline.

"Bill," he said, "do everything you can to meet that schedule. I don't want to be the first one of the Logistics Centers to request a delay."

"But General, sooner or later it's going to be obvious," I said.

"It isn't going to be obvious as long as I'm here," he replied.

The General did not want to be the first to deliver bad news to Wright-Patterson. The basic problem with the ALS as designed was that it was way ahead of its time. It was beyond state-of-the-art technology and demanded more time to develop than was initially allotted. It was eventually implemented, but not to the sophisticated degree we had originally planned.

When General Ridell retired, his replacement, General Jack, did not fully understand all of the aspects of the software development or the pilot program, nor did he fully realize their importance. In his opinion, it was just one of his many responsibilities.

At the same time, the work at Kelly I thought would be less stressful was becoming more stressful than even my previous assignment at Wright-Patterson. Deadlines were quickly approaching, which were not going to be met. I finally decided I could not properly manage my responsibilities as Director of Computer Services and at the same time take care of my family as well as I wanted.

I began to think of retirement, however, I wanted an assignment that would provide a transition into civilian life. I applied to U.S. Air Force Headquarters to direct the ROTC program at Arizona State University in Tempe, Arizona. My mandatory retirement was set for November 1974. Due to that short duration of only a year and a half, I was turned down. My idea was to complete my military career in ROTC and then teach at the university.

When that transfer was turned down, I decided to retire. I had the 30 years of service necessary for maximum retirement pay since my inactive reserve time counted for retirement. When I discussed it with my Commanding General, he accepted my decision.

My decision was based primarily on my desire to spend more time with Marilyn and the children. It was the classic

CERTIFICATE OF RETIREMENT
FROM THE ARMED FORCES OF THE UNITED STATES OF AMERICA

TO ALL WHO SHALL SEE THESE PRESENTS, GREETING
THIS IS TO CERTIFY THAT

Col Louis W. Cracken

HAVING SERVED FAITHFULLY AND HONORABLY
WAS RETIRED FROM THE

UNITED STATES AIR FORCE

ON THE *First* DAY OF *April*
ONE THOUSAND NINE HUNDRED AND *Seventy Three*

JACK J. CATTON General, USAF
Commander, Air Force Logistics Command

CHIEF OF STAFF

trade-off between work and family, and, as I had before, I chose family.

Instead of waiting for compulsory retirement in November 1974, I retired in April 1973. As a senior full Colonel, I was entitled to a farewell parade. I declined the honor. I did, however, enjoy the casual farewell party thrown by my Branch Chiefs and my staff.

I was awarded seven decorations with Oak Leaf Clusters during the course of my military career, as well as Presidential Unit Citations from the United States, the Philippines, and Korea. In addition, I am qualified to wear four battle stars on my World War II Pacific Theater Ribbon and four battle stars on my Korean War Theater Ribbon, as well as assorted other ribbons such as the Sharpshooter Ribbon. I was proud of my service in the Air Force, having on all occasions done the very best I could. I always tried to take care of the people who worked with me and for me.

I had also always tried to take care of my family while I was in the service. But at the end of my time at Kelly, I was relieved to know I truly would be able to spend more time with them. It was both a sad and happy occasion.

After slightly over 30 years, I was now a civilian.

Improving on Government

Afterward

When I retired, I didn't have any particular future in mind. My Colonel's pension was enough to support my family, but at 53 and in excellent health, I wanted to work.

Teaching still appealed to me. I had enjoyed teaching in the Air Force and at Maryland State College, so initially, I applied for a professorship in Management with San Antonio Community College. My first teaching assignment was at Randolph Air Force Base at night. In view of wanting to spend time with Marilyn and the children, I didn't want to teach at night, so I turned it down. There was no certainty of a day assignment in the future.

About the same time, my friend Jim Bailey, who was my superior and a good friend in England, and now President of Troy State University's satellite campus in Montgomery, Alabama, offered me a position as an Assistant Professor. I traveled to Troy State to interview and was approved for a contract as Assistant Professor of Management. The job was appealing enough for me to return to Montgomery with Marilyn to look for houses. It was an extremely competitive housing market, in part because Montgomery is the home of Maxwell Air Force Base as well as being Alabama's state capital. The lack of an acceptable house coupled with the intense summer humidity, which aggravated Marilyn's health problems, led me to disappoint my friend and again decline a position.

Following up on a newspaper ad, I applied to teach management courses at Our Lady of the Lake University near Kelly Air Force Base. Again I was offered only one night position at Kelly, but since Kelly was closer to home than Randolph, I did teach one semester while looking for a more interesting opportunity.

Shortly after that I learned from a friend at Wright-Patterson who was working closely with the Iranian Air Force that there was an opening in Iran for a Deputy Director of Aircraft Maintenance and Engineering for the Iranian Air Force. They were looking for an American with the right background, and an interviewer was coming to San Antonio. The interviewer was a retired civil servant I knew from Wright-Patterson. He immediately said he knew I was qualified for the position, and I could have it if I wanted it. I would be the Deputy and advisor to an Iranian General. The Iranians were building an extremely large depot, and their intent was to duplicate the operations at Kelly.

John and Rachel were teenagers at the time, and Marilyn's health was still a consideration. So, before traveling to California for several weeks of briefing prior to leaving for Iran, I began to investigate the living arrangements there. I had presumed we would have a villa with servants and a car. The kids would go to school in Europe, paid for in full by the Iranians. It was a three-year contract with a two-week, all-expenses-paid trip to Europe annually, as well as a trip back to the United States every year. At the end of the third year, after successful completion of the assignment, and, if I did not wish to continue, the Iranian government would pay me a substantial bonus.

Through my investigation, however, I discovered some of

my presumptions were wrong. We would actually live in a compound, not a villa. I could not drive my own car, but would have to rely upon a driver. Quality health-care for Marilyn was in question. And I really didn't like the idea of the kids being abroad at school. Quickly I determined the job and the living situation were far too restrictive, so I declined the position. My timing could not have been better. A short time later, civil war broke out, the Shah was forced to leave the country, and some Americans were taken hostage.

While looking around, I took MBA courses at a University of Texas at San Antonio satellite facility near our house. I enjoyed the classes tremendously. One of my professors was Henry Cisneros, who would soon be Mayor of San Antonio and later Secretary of HUD under President Bill Clinton. The Air Force paid for the classes since I had never used up my GI Bill credits.

In 1975, I was taking the last two courses for my MBA when I heard about a job opportunity with Datapoint Corporation. The job conflicted with the courses, so I never completed the degree.

Datapoint was a growing corporation in the late '70s and a pioneer in the design, integration, and maintenance of data, voice, and video communications solutions. The company is known as an inventor of many noteworthy technologies, including the Local Area Network (LAN). At the time I joined on, it was doubling its sales every other year. Due to my industrial engineering background, I was initially assigned as a Scheduler for incoming orders. Soon after I joined the company, my boss was reassigned and I became the Master Scheduler. After numerous reorganizations, I became first Manager and then Director of Production Planning and Master Scheduler and reported to the Vice President for Manufacturing, Vic Palermo.

The company's stock price depended upon continuous growth. To accomplish this, Datapoint executives planned a growth curve for the coming year with quarterly goals. The company recorded revenues when an item shipped, not when

Afterward

the product was delivered or when the payment was received. When the desired level of revenues for each quarter was reached, shipments were halted for the rest of the quarter. A backlog then accumulated and was shipped the first week of the next quarter. The idea behind this practice was to boost revenues for the following quarter.

If actual shipments lagged and more revenues were needed to meet the projected quarterly goal, the company shipped units ahead of desired delivery dates. When customers balked, Datapoint paid for product storage until the customer needed the product. Using a statistical forecasting tool, I was able to better predict what customers really needed, resulting in a more accurate finished goods inventory at the end of each quarter.

Datapoint was a high-tech company trying hard to handle growth. I spent as much as 70 percent of my time and energy getting new products out on schedule. This proved to be a problem. In high technology, product development and delivery are critical. Datapoint began to slip behind its competitors by allowing new key products to sometimes lag behind in shipping. If you slip behind too much, your customers may eventually leave you for companies with better and more sophisticated products. This is what was happening to Datapoint.

In April 1980, I asked for a six-week leave of absence. It was our 25th wedding anniversary, and I wanted to take Marilyn on an extensive tour of England and Scotland. This was an unprecedented request at Datapoint since my job was a critical, day-to-day position. Management was reluctant, but I told them they could give me the time off or I would quit. They finally agreed.

By the time I got back from our trip—a wonderful excursion with our friends and neighbors Bert and Patti Young—I realized that Datapoint had become a pressure-prone position. Again I found myself working 10- and 12-hour days, as well as going in on the weekends. I was the oldest of the executives. The others were all young and ambitious, but I was just doing something to keep busy. Finally, I was no longer willing to accept the pressure of the position. Datapoint wanted me to stay. I was one of the few employees there over 50 and they were sensitive to increasing pressure from Congress to practice fair employment. When I left, they gave me a generous three-month bonus, unusual for people voluntarily resigning. I retired in August 1980.

Retirement gave me more time to spend on the civic and personal interests I had adopted while in San Antonio, including serving on the board of the Victoria Courts Child Care Center, the largest child-care center in San Antonio. I was a member of the board for six years, the last two years as Vice President. They had asked me to serve as President, but I declined because I didn't want to take the time away from my family. Presidency to me means running the organization. The same thing happened at the San Antonio Little Theatre Board. I was on the board there for five years, the last two years as Vice President and declined the presidency. I was also active

Christmas 1979. John, Rachel, Bill, and Marilyn.

in the University Club, a club of professionals representing various fields that included several Generals and university Presidents. I was on the board of the University Club, were I was proud just to be a member, for four years. In the second year, I was elected Vice President, and I also served as Acting President for six months. For two years I was on the board of the local chapter of the Multiple Sclerosis Society. When I resigned, Marilyn took over.

Marilyn and I also became sponsors of the Christian Children's Fund worldwide, giving monthly to sponsor first a boy from Brazil and later a little girl. Even before we were married, helping children had been something that had captured my interest. I had years earlier assisted a young Navajo Indian boy in Arizona through the Save The Children Federation.

Marilyn and I have also made it a practice to help people directly when we can. We once met a young lady named Barbara through an MS support group that Marilyn headed up. She was divorced and had two small children. Her vehicle broke down and she was dropped from her job. She was desperate. I called a Ford dealer in San Antonio, Red McCombs, who, by the way, owns the Minnesota Vikings football team. I talked with his personal secretary and discussed Barbara's situation. She was very interested and promised to talk to her boss. She called me back and told me to see one of their service managers. He was a former Marine and we became friendly. He told me if we brought her vehicle down there, he would service it for free. Bill Banis, who owned a local service station, volunteered to tow Barbara's car to the Ford agency. It cost over $2,000 to repair the vehicle, at no cost to Barbara thanks to Red McCombs. With a dependable car to drive, she was able to get her job back.

We became acquainted with a young blind lady named Hope through our daughter Rachel and her husband, Paul. Hope and Paul had been at Indiana University together. She later separated from her husband and moved to San Antonio

3510 Quiver Drive
San Antonio, TX 78238
March 14, 1990

Mr. Red McCombs
Red McCombs Automotive Center
P.O. Box BH003
San Antonio, TX 78201

Dear Mr. McCombs:

May I take this means of thanking Dan Agnew, Mike Charbeneau and
Joe Boyle and most of all yourself for the generous and humane act of
providing and installing a complete car engine and other necessary
service to Mrs. Barbara Green's Ford Tempo, at no expense to her.

Mrs. Green is a mother with two very small children who is separated
from her husband and living on a very limited income provided by him.
A Multiple Sclerosis victim she was until recently the chairperson of
a Multiple Sclerosis support group unselfishly giving of herself to
others with the same problem. Separation from her husband and the
inability to seek employment, without a car, made it impossible for
her to continue. My wife, Marilyn, and I can not think of anyone
more worthy of being helped than Barbara. Marilyn, who also has
Multiple Sclerosis, was a member of her group and now chairs another
support group. Now that Barbara needs help herself we have taken it
upon ourselves to help her in any way we can.

This thank you letter is written on behalf of Mrs. Green, the local
chapter of the National Multiple Sclerosis Society and the Crackens.
Please be assured that we are all most grateful for your generosity
and compassion and that your action will give Mrs. Green a chance,
with a working car, to retain her dignity and the ability and seek
employment to support herself and her little girl and boy.

May I thank you and the gentlemen named above for myself, and for
what it is worth, add my name to your fans and that of your Ford Agency
and the SPURS.

With my best wishes,

Most gratefully,

WILLIAM CRACKEN

*Dan,
Thanks for all of your help. Cell me at your convenience.
By the way, I am an Industrial Engineer. If can ever be of help, I am at your service, No fee.
Bill*

with her two children. She worked for Child Protective Services (CPS), but was in a difficult position there since she needed special attention and a special computer. One day her little boy went to school with some scratches on his face and the teacher asked him how it happened. Somehow he implied that his mother was involved, and she misunderstood and reported the incident to CPS.

It got back to the head of Hope's department and she fired

her. Marilyn and I had been helping Hope acclimate. I was indignant about the situation and enlisted the help of a friend, County Judge Cindi Krier. She mentioned the situation to a friend who was a state senator. I wrote Governor Ann Richards, and we began to elevate the visibility of the injustice. Ultimately, the state paid Hope $50,000 in damages and she found a new job through the Commission for the Blind with the U.S. Treasury Department. She was transferred to St. Louis where she spent the money to buy a condominium. Eventually, she reconciled with her husband and the family is doing well. We continue to send birthday presents to her children every year.

There are many other instances, but I will mention just a couple more. Marilyn goes to physical therapy regularly, and we got to know a young boy there named Wesley who has spina bifida. We learned that Wesley's parents couldn't afford the therapy and that he would soon not be coming back. Marilyn and I happily picked up the responsibility of paying for this needed care.

In the late '80s, Marilyn and I had just returned to San Antonio after visiting our son, John, in Dallas, and had decided to stop at Jim's, a coffee shop near the airport, for dinner before going home. I watched a family—a mother, daughter, and son—near our table. The son was very active and playful with his mother. He obviously loved her very much and reminded me of a story my mother had told me not long before she died. As the story goes, a little boy was in the park picking up leaves in the fall and trying to put them back on the trees. A gentleman came along and asked the boy why he was doing this. The boy told him, "The doctor told my mother that when all the leaves in the park had fallen, she would die." The story ends with the gentleman paying for the mother to go south to a warmer climate.

I called the little boy over and gave him $5 and told him to spend it any way he wanted. He was thrilled.

After he walked back to his table, Marilyn suggested we give something to the little girl, too. So I called the little boy

1997. Cliff, a fine young man.

back over to the table and offered another $5 for his sister.

To my surprise, he replied, "No, thank you. I will share the money you gave me with her."

This really touched me. On the way out, we sat down and talked with the family at length. The mother was divorced. The boy, Cliff, was six at the time. He is 16 now. Since that day 10 years ago, Marilyn and I have "adopted" Cliff and his family. Cliff now lives in Harlingen, in the Rio Grande Valley, near Brownsville, Texas. Nevertheless, two or three times a year, his mother drives him up to San Antonio to spend time with us. We are in constant communication by phone, letter, or e-mail. Recently, Cliff's English teacher asked him to write an essay about a person he most admired who had been a great influence on him. I was very touched when Cliff told me he chose me.

I've been very lucky in my life. Marilyn has chronic progressive MS, which can worsen slowly. Her condition is really almost the same as it was when we first came to San Antonio. She now walks with a cane and uses a three-wheeled collapsible cart when we go out to stay mobile. An electric cart takes her on longer trips around town. We put it on an airplane with us and go everywhere. At home, she has a four-wheeled cart. We have not moved for 28 years despite a couple of false

Summer 1995. With Marilyn in Horseshoe Bay, Texas.

starts and much prompting from our children because the house accommodates Marilyn better than any other we've found.

Both of my children have done well. My daughter lives in San Antonio with her husband, Paul, an educator, and their sons, Robert and William. My son, John, is a graduate of the University of Texas and its law school. He is now a senior partner in a law firm and is a partner in a company that acquires businesses. He and his wife, Heather, have a daughter,

Marilyn, a son, Eric, and are expecting another child.

Once I decided to fully retire, my thoughts turned to looking after my family and to my interest in political science, an area I had put on the back burner. I have always been puzzled why the advances in the physical sciences have far exceeded advances in the political sciences. It should take the same in-

Christmas 1997. The Cracken Clan in Texas.

telligence to make progress in both. Yet today, we have scientific marvels undreamed of at the turn of the century, but nations are still fighting nations—and our political system is still struggling with basically the same problems we faced 100 years ago.

Is this not the time, as we approach the 21st century, to take an inventory of where we are and where we would like to be in the future?

Afterward

For the last few years, I have been writing down on five-by-eight-inch cards (I now have over 2,000), ideas on how to improve our political system, which I will someday use in a book. Most of them are copied from one source or another. Few of them are original. I consider the following quote particularly relevant:

"A Democracy cannot exist as a permanent form of government. It can exist only until the voters discover that they can vote themselves largesse from the public treasury. From that moment on, the majority always votes for candidates promising the most benefits from the public treasury, with the result that a Democracy always collapses over loose fiscal policy, always followed by a Dictatorship.

"The average age of the world's greatest civilizations has been 200 years. These nations have progressed through this sequence: From bondage to spiritual faith; from spiritual faith to great courage; from courage to liberty; from liberty to abundance; from abundance to selfishness; from selfishness to complacency; from complacency to apathy; from apathy to dependency; from dependency back into bondage."

This passage was written by Professor Alexander Tyler in 1776 while the original 13 U.S. colonies were still part of the British dominion. He was writing about the fall of the Athenian Republic more than 2,000 years earlier.

A summary of the theme of my book is as follows:

My idea is to publish a nonfiction, politically oriented book offering specific ideas for changes that would make our government better managed and thus better able to compete in the 21st century. Today, most books of this type concentrate on what's wrong and its impact, occasionally offering parochial solutions. This book will be holistic in nature, and it will address (1) the people and how to make them more vigilant, (2) the leaders and how to improve their quality and ability to govern, and (3) the structure and laws and how we can make both better meet our ideals of a benevolent democracy.

The goal is to make this country more secure, with a sound economy and social justice for all. Thus, a society prepared to lead the world into the 21st century and beyond. The solutions offered are mostly not new and, though feasible and having merit, have not been adequately presented to the public. All are at the very least thought provoking. I know of no current book whose theme is the consolidation of specific solutions across a wide spectrum of political activities. The book will include chapters on foreign relations, the economy, justice, social programs, national defense, government structure, public enlightenment, selection of leaders, natural resources and ecology, as well as a number of others. It will also contain a unique feature related to the public's opportunity to voice their views and suggest their own solutions.

As a retired business executive, a military officer, and an academic, both my education and experience included observing our political environment closely and for quite a number of years. I know we can do better. In fact, we better do better as we approach the 21st century and its unpredictable challenges, changes, and threats. There is no one now and in the near future who can pick up our torch of leadership of the free world. We must be prepared to lead into the 21st century and beyond. I am motivated by the hope that this project may in its small way play a modest part. The potential is unlimited.

One example of an idea that will be included in the book in the chapter on better leaders is quoted here:

"Establish a 'national academy' chartered by the U.S. Government to annually publicly honor American citizens who perform outstanding service to our country or humanity. Honorees would become life members of the academy. A committee appointed by the President would select initial membership. The academy members would select subsequent membership. Annually, the new honorees would be recognized at a ball held in Washington, hopefully the most important national social event, chaired by the President. The event would receive the widest news media coverage and should more than rival in importance and prestige the Queen's Honors List and the Nobel Prizes. Each honoree would receive a medal on a chain as a member of the august academy and the title of e.g.

Afterward

'Companion of Merit' with the privilege of adding 'C.M.' after his or her name. Hopefully, the C.M. designation would eventually carry a greater distinction than any other honor this country has to give, and also receive worldwide recognition. Foreign nationals could also be honored and receive associate membership (non-participating). Regular members would become associate members upon reaching a prescribed age or when unable or unwilling to serve as active members.

The academy's functions would include, but not be limited to: (1) annually selecting new members, (2) advising the President in their professional capacity or as a corporate body, and (3) acting as centers of influence in their areas for local or national civic or political improvements. If properly established, administered, and nurtured, the academy could be an unprecedented positive force for good, both as a corporate body and as individuals, inspiring millions of Americans, young and old, now and in the future. The academy would be an instrument for the recognition of genuine heroes and, to the young, worthwhile people to emulate and respect. The news media could feature the honorees and their accomplishments, thus reducing space and time currently allocated to sordid and sensational subjects and to the glorification of pseudo-heroes filling a vacuum. The entire fabric of American life could be lifted. The 'Medal of Freedom' currently awarded by the U.S. Government falls somewhat short of this program."

If any reader of this book would like to initiate a dialogue with me on my personal experiences, political science in general, or my idea for the proposed book, I would welcome the opportunity to do so. My e-mail address is bcracken@onramp.net.

It is my view that there are very rare occasions today when war, avoidable human suffering, or poor political leadership should be considered unavoidable or tolerated. In the near future, human intelligence, able to create the modern miracles of technology, can and should demand applying the necessary priority and resources to the challenges of making all of the above not rare but always avoidable and never tolerated.

When I was a little boy, I read *The Story of Mankind* by Hendrik Van Loon, a bestseller at that time. In his epilogue, he offered a prayer " ... that someday men would find a way to live with each other in peace, and that the men who would find the way would be blessed throughout the ages ...". Even then, his words touched my heart, and, to this day, I have not forgotten them. While I enjoyed reading about the flying aces of World War I and dreamed the impossible dream of being one of those men, today Van Loon's prayer is just as important and real to me—even after a lifelong career in the military. My boyhood dream was just a dream, but I have not given up. I can still hope that someday, a member of my family may play a part in that dream.

On a personal note and in conclusion, I would like to explain, hopefully not as an excuse, that it was difficult for me, as a very private person, to fully express my emotions in this book. It is the reason I did not want to write it. As an orphan at an early age, I trained myself to avoid emotions and control my feelings. I think it was a mixed blessing, helping me to remain cool and calm under adverse conditions, yet handicapping me in my personal relations. It made me hesitate to commit myself and, for example, delayed my decision to marry Marilyn and start a family beyond a reasonable time. I feel I am fortunate to have partially overcome this personal hang-up in that I have a very warm and close relationship with my family and I have made many lifelong friends.

Perhaps there are better mottoes to live by. Certainly mine is not original. "Grace under Pressure," to me, means a great deal more than these simple words express. Grace embodies among other attributes honor and service.

My very best wishes to each reader.